aurora
guides

Hermitage

Hermitage

AN ILLUSTRATED GUIDE

AURORA ART PUBLISHERS
LENINGRAD

Selection and text by
YURI SHAPIRO

Translated from the Russian by
ARTHUR SHKAROVSKY-RAFFÉ

Designed by
YURI DYSHLENKO

Front illustration:
Raphael. *The Conestabile Madonna.* Detail

Frontispiece:
Small Hermitage: Pavilion Hall. Detail

Back illustration:
Winter Palace

Э $\frac{4903010000\text{-}322}{023(01)\text{-}83}$ 161-83

LIST OF CONTENTS

The˘ Hermitage Museum: Buildings and Rooms 7

A Culture and Art of Classical Antiquity 30

  Ancient Greece 32
  Ancient Rome 41

W Western European Art 45

  Italian Art: 13th—20th Centuries . . . 48
  Spanish Art: 15th—Early 19th Centuries 70
  Western European Arms and Armour: 15th—17th Centuries 78
  Netherlandish Art: 15th—Early 17th Centuries 79
  Flemish Art: 17th Century 83
  Dutch Art: 17th Century 94
  German Art: 15th—19th Centuries . . . 105
  French Art: 15th—20th Centuries . . . 110
  English Art: 17th—19th Centuries . . . 155

E Culture and Art of the Peoples of the East . . . 159

  Ancient Egypt 162
  China 168
  India 176
  Byzantium 178
  Iran 183
  Central Asia 186
  Urartu 189

P   **History of Primitive Culture** 190

     Artefacts Found in the USSR 192

     Culture and Art of the Scythians . . . 193

     Culture and Art of the Sarmatians . . . 197

     Cultural Relics of Southern Siberia . . . 198

R   **History of Russian Culture** 200

     Late 17th and Early 18th Centuries . . 202

     Middle and Second Half of the 18th Century 205

     List of the Hermitage Departments . . . 212

     Index of Names 214

NOTE: The bold-type letters indicate the names of corresponding sections in the floor-plans. Given in parentheses after the title of each reproduced exhibit is the plate number followed by the capital letter indicating its section and the number of the room where it is displayed.

The Hermitage Museum: Buildings and Rooms

The buildings of the State Hermitage Museum (1), the largest repository of world-famous art treasures in the Soviet Union, are magnificent monuments of art in their own right, created by a succession of eminent architects. The Museum complex consists of five buildings which are lined along the Neva, Leningrad's main waterway, beginning with the Winter Palace near the Palace Bridge and ending with the Hermitage Theatre.

The Hermitage's foundation date is considered the year 1764, when 225 canvases bought by Catherine II from the German merchant Johann Ernest Gotzkowsky were delivered to the Winter Palace. Since then it has grown from a small picture gallery in the palace of the Russian Empress into a major museum and an important research and educational centre. Today the Hermitage is visited by about three and a half million people annually. During the Soviet period the museum collections have increased more than fourfold.

The museum comprises six major departments dealing with primitive culture, classical antiquities, culture and art of the peoples of the East, Western European art, Russian culture, and numismatics. Their collections, arranged in 330 rooms, contain over 2,700,000 items.

Winter Palace (2)

The visitor will gain his first impression of the Museum when he stops to admire the Winter Palace, its main building, which presents a particularly striking view from Palace Square or from the Neva embankment. The solemn rhythm of its colonnades is full of majestic harmony; the silhouetted statues on the roof-top, etched distinctly against the sky, extend the verticals of the columns above the broken line of the cornices; the alternating recesses and projections of the building, its diverse colonnades, the effect of light and shade on the jagged outlines of the façades, decked out in three different colours — all these features play their part in creating the dynamic and festive external appearance of the Palace.

8

One cold winter day in 1837 the Palace's overheated stoves burst into
flames that, after raging for three days, left nothing but the charred
shell of the original building put up in 1754—62 by the famous architect Francesco Bartolommeo Rastrelli (1700—1771). Due to the efforts
of the eminent architect Vasily Stasov (1769—1848) and some 8,000
workmen that he commanded, the Palace was completely restored to its
original state within a mere two years.

Main Staircase (3)

When re-creating the Jordan Staircase — now called the Main Staircase
as it is the chief entrance to the Museum — Stasov echoed Rastrelli's
objective of designing a ceremonial entrance on so grand a scale that it

would immediately impress the visitor by its opulent majesty. It is indeed staggering in its dimensions and splendour, enhanced by the glittering wall mirrors, which, by their reflection of the windows, further increase the effect of spaciousness. After the first flight of steps — of the same brilliant creamy Carrara marble as the hand-rails — the stairs fork in two broad sweeps to right and left. Rising up imposingly above the first-floor balustrade is an elegant colonnade of grey Serdobolye granite; here the eye is caught by the huge plafond, which at the soaring height of twenty-two metres makes the ceiling seem much higher than it really is. The plafond depicting the gods on Olympus was painted to a design by the Italian Gasparo Tiziani. The sumptuous, elaborate décor is further augmented by graceful statues of mythological deities and the Rococo strapwork ornament of gilded alabaster and plaster.

Memorial Room of Peter the Great (4, R-194) and Armorial Hall (5, R-195)

The Memorial Room of Peter the Great (formerly the Small Throne Room) was designed in 1833 by the architect Auguste Montferrand (1786—1858) and restored after the 1837 conflagration by Stasov almost

exactly as before. Along the upper part of the walls in this second room
are panels painted in tempera on canvas by the Italian artists Barnaba
Medici and Pietro Scotti and depicting the Emperor at the famous Battle
of Poltava (1709). Between columns of jasper in the large central niche
hangs a painting of Peter the Great with Minerva, the work of the Venetian painter Jacopo Amigoni. The silver-gilt Imperial throne was made
in England in 1731 by Nicholas Klausen of fumed oak.

The large Armorial Hall (its floorspace is 1,000 square metres) served as
the venue for ceremonial receptions. It was decorated by Stasov with a
Corinthian colonnade and a balustraded gallery along the perimeter;
its chandeliers are ornamented with escutcheons displaying the armorial bearings of the old Russian provinces.

War Gallery (6, R-197)

In 1826 Carlo Rossi (1775—1849) designed a picture gallery to display
332 portraits — by the well-known English portrait painter George Dawe
(1781—1829) and the two Russian artists Alexander Poliakov (1801—
1835) and Vasily Golike (1802—1848) — of Russian and Allied generals
who fought Napoleon during the war of 1812—14. Central is Dawe's
portrait of Field-marshal Mikhail Golenishchev-Kutuzov (7, R-197), the
Commander-in-Chief of Russia's armies, who is depicted against snow-
swept plains across which troops are marching. Other fine and highly

6

expressive portraits — of Barclay de Tolly, Bagration, Denis Davydov, Seslavin, Uvarov and Yermolov — eloquently convey the mood of heroic uplift characteristic of the period.

Of an entirely different nature are the pictures at the end of the gallery where the immense equestrian portrait of the Russian Emperor Alexander I hangs. Its author, Franz Krüger (1797—1859), assiduously but without feeling portrayed both the arrogantly-looking rider and his mount, with an equal abundance of meticulous detail. Similarly unimpassioned are the two ceremonially hieratic portraits of King Friedrich Wilhelm III of Prussia, again by Krüger, and of the Austrian Emperor Franz I, by Peter Krafft (1780—1856).

Undertaking to restore the Gallery after the 1837 fire — all the portraits had fortunately been got out in time — Stasov adhered almost entirely to Rossi's original concept, only slightly extending the Gallery in length and adding a small gallery above the cornice.

St. George Hall (8, R-198)

When designing the St. George Hall (originally called the Great Throne Room), Stasov strove to impart to it an air of austere majesty, by means of just two colours — white and gold. Indeed, the white Carrara marble used for the columns, the walls, the low relief of St. George, a symbol

of Russia's might, and the white ceiling offer a striking contrast to
the glittering ormolu mounts of the immense chandeliers, the gilded
capitals and bases of the columns and details of the gallery balusters.
The ceiling décor of embossed bronze, also gilded, faithfully repro-
duces — with the exception of a few minor details — the design of the
parquet flooring made up of sixteen different types of wood.
Stasov also devised a highly original construction, whose reliability has
stood the test of time: he used only metal for a ceiling of 800 square

8

metres in area. The iron girders and sheets of copper — painted white on the underside — were anchored in place by two ship's chains.

Where the Imperial throne once stood is now a mosaic map of the USSR, twenty-seven square metres in area, assembled by craftsmen of the Peterhof Lapidary Works near Leningrad from 45,000 semi-precious stones mined in this country. It was displayed at the Paris World Exhibition in 1937, where it was awarded a Grand Prix, and again at the 1939 international exhibition in New York.

**Malachite Room (9, R-189) and
Private Dining Room (10, R-188)**

The Malachite Room, designed in 1838—39 by the architect Alexander
Briullov, has no parallel in the world, with — as the name implies —
malachite facing columns and pilasters, and adorning mantlepieces and
furniture. The decoration of the room took over 2,000 kilogrammes of
malachite. Gilding was also used on a wide scale, mainly for the mould-
ings of bronze capitals and the bases of columns. Ormolu decorates
mantelpieces, mirror frames and papier-mâché moulded designs covering
the major part of the ceiling. An original and effective blend of two
materials, bright-green malachite and glistening gold, gives the interior
an air of magnificence and splendour. The impression is enhanced by a
beautiful parquet floor made up of nine different kinds of wood.

The Malachite Room and its neighbouring Private Dining Room are directly associated with the stirring events of the October Revolution of
1917 in Petrograd — as St. Petersburg was renamed after the outbreak
of the First World War. In July 1917 the bourgeois Provisional Government took over the Malachite Room as the venue for cabinet meetings.
After the Winter Palace was stormed on 25 October (7 November, New
Style), 1917, the revolutionary Red Guards, soldiers and sailors, arrested
the Ministers of the Provisional Government in the Private Dining Room,
to which they had retired when the assault began. This historic event
occurred at ten past two in the morning of 26 October (8 November).

11, 12   **Small Hermitage (11): Pavilion Hall (12, W-204)
and Hanging Garden (14)**

Erected in 1764—75 and adjoining the eastern end of the Winter Palace
is a typical group of eighteenth-century pavilions known as the Small
Hermitage, the name deriving from the French *ermitage*, a place of
seclusion. Built by the two architects, Yuri Velten (1730—1801) and
Jean-Baptiste Vallin de la Mothe (1729—1800), it has two galleries that
link the North Pavilion, on the Neva embankment side, with the South
Pavilion.

On the North Pavilion's first floor, originally of seven rooms and a
glass-enclosed conservatory with evergreens and uncaged birds, the architect Andrei Stakenschneider (1802—1865) constructed what is known
as the Pavilion Hall. Though somewhat eclectic in style, combining elements of Renaissance and Mauritan art, with graceful galleries resting
on elegant marble columns and the floor decorated by a half-size copy
of an ancient Roman mosaic, nonetheless the interior décor represents
a cohesive whole.

13, 14

A notable curio displayed here is the Peacock Clock (13, W-204), the work of James Cox, a leading eighteenth-century English clockmaker. The hours and minutes are indicated in the windows cut out in the cap of a mushroom, and when the chimes play the peacock spreads its plumage and nods, the owl blinks and turns its head, and the cock crows. The highly intricate, bizarre mechanism is in full working order.

On one side the windows overlook the Neva, on the other, the Hanging Garden, which is situated between the Eastern and Western galleries above the former Imperial stables and coach houses.

The rooms adjacent to the Hanging Garden already contained a number of art treasures, which had been purchased abroad, as early as the eighteenth century. In 1764 the Berlin merchant Johann Gotzkowsky sent to St. Petersburg a collection of 225 paintings as repayment of his outstanding debts, and that year is thus considered to have been the date of the foundation of the Hermitage collection. This nucleus was systematically added to by the purchase of more works of art, indeed of entire collections such as those of Count Karl Kobentzl from Brussels in 1768, of Count Heinrich Brühl from Dresden in the following year, of the Marquis de Crozat from Paris in 1772, of Lord Walpole, the British Prime Minister, in 1779, and of Count François Baudoin from Paris, two years later. In short, by 1785 the Hermitage already had a collection of 2,658 paintings.

15, 16

**Old Hermitage (15): Leonardo Room (16, W-214)
Hermitage Theatre: Raphael Loggias**

In 1771—87, to house the many new acquisitions, another building, now known as the Old Hermitage, was erected, again by Velten, next to the Small Hermitage on the Neva embankment. In the middle of the nineteenth century the architect Stackenschneider designed there a room in imitation of stately palace interiors. The décor of the room, where paintings by Leonardo are now displayed, widely employs expensive and highly decorative materials — marble, striated jasper, lapis lazuli, rare kinds of wood, gilt bronze and tortoise-shell (the latter is used for the doors adorned in the Boulle technique). The upper part of the walls and the ceiling are decorated with picturesque panels and a plafond painted by Academician Fiodor Bruni.

In the last four years of construction the architect conceived and executed the then daring project of spanning the Winter Canal with an arched passageway between the two buildings.

The Hermitage Theatre was built in 1783—86 by Giacomo Quarenghi (1744—1817) — although the façade was completed only in 1802. Later on in the nineteenth century the auditorium was somewhat modified while the exterior of the building remained as before. The foyer was designed by Leonty Benois (1856—1928) in 1904.

In the 1780s Giacomo Quarenghi erected along the Winter Canal a gallery similar to Bramante's celebrated structure at the Vatican. Its walls

were hung with copies, in tempera on canvas, of the world-famous frescoes that Raphael and his pupils executed for the Vatican's Raphael Loggias.

The acquisition of diverse collections continued in the nineteenth century. Thus paintings from Empress Josephine's Malmaison Palace were purchased in 1814, the Marquis de Campana collection of antiquities was acquired in 1861, examples of the Byzantine applied arts from the Anton Basilewski collection were bought in 1884—85; and a collection of Western European arms and armour was transferred to the Hermitage from the Tsarskoye Selo Arsenal in 1885. Individual works of art were also purchased.

New Hermitage (17): Large Skylight Room (18, W-238)

In 1850 the architects Vasily Stasov and Nikolai Yefimov (1799—1851) completed the erection, after a design by Leo von Klenze, of the New Hermitage, built specially as a museum of fifty-six rooms to display both Russian and Western European works of art. Its portico is held by ten figures of atlantes carved of granite by the Russian sculptor Alexander Terebenev (1815—1859).

Leo von Klenze designed three more halls, notably Rooms 237—239, with the express purpose of mounting a collection of paintings therein. This explains the complete absence of windows, which was to increase

wallspace for the hanging of pictures, as well as the use of skylights to provide for evenly diffused lighting and the use of a uniform colour for the walls so as not to distract the viewer from the pictures on display. However, the ceilings are richly ornamented with stucco moulding, gilding and relief medallions.

Although on 7 February 1852 the Museum was announced as open to the public, special viewing permits were required; hence in the course of a

year no more than 500 people actually saw this collection. Only from 1863 did the Museum become open to all.

During the First World War the Hermitage collections were evacuated to Moscow, whence returned to the Museum after the October Revolution of 1917. Today the total number of exhibits in the Hermitage collection amounts to over 2,700,000 items with displays held in 400 rooms, while the total annual attendance has already topped 3,400,000.

 # Culture and Art of Classical Antiquity

The Hermitage's collection of classical antiquities, the finest and largest in the Soviet Union, includes over 113,000 items, and, more specifically, vast and varied assemblages of ancient Greek pottery, gems and Roman marbles. The displays in question are mounted in ground-floor Rooms 106—109, 111—118, 120, 121 and 127—131. Some of these premises were specially added in the nineteenth century to exhibit various collections of antiquities, a fact reflected in both their design and interior décor. For example, Room 108 resembles a peristyle of the type found in ancient Rome, with a row of columns surrounding an open area, and displayed there are the decorative sculptures that adorned such courtyards.

Meanwhile Room 130, otherwise known as the Hall of Twenty Columns, attracts attention not only by its monolithic granite columns and floor mosaics but also because of its wall paintings on classical motifs, each of which depicts, among other objects, vessels similar to the artefacts exhibited beneath them. The walls of several other rooms have been plastered with tinted stucco, which serves as an excellent background for the ancient marbles on display.

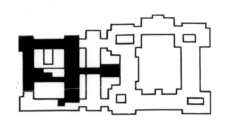

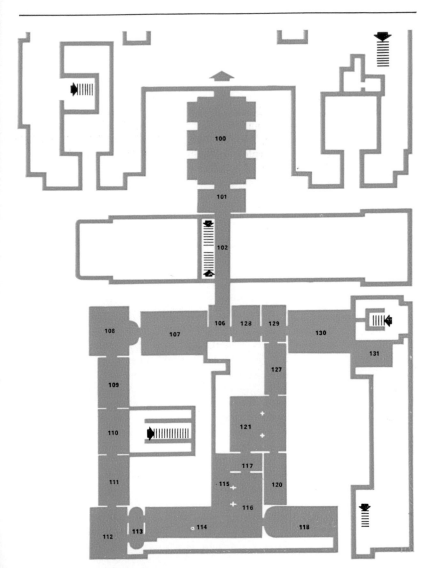

CULTURE AND ART OF ANCIENT GREECE

Vases

The Hermitage collection of ancient vases is one of the largest in the world, and its finest specimens give the visitor a good idea of pottery-making in various centres between the ninth and third century B.C.

Of note among works, which illustrate an early stage in Greece's trade links with the tribes inhabiting the Crimea and adjacent areas, is a **A** beautiful vessel for wine, oinochoe (21, A-114). Made in Asia Minor in the seventh century B.C. and discovered in a Scythian burial of the sixth century B.C. near Kerch (Temir-Gora barrow), the vessel is executed in the so-called carpet style.

The red-figure style, which appeared at the turn of the sixth and fifth centuries B.C., is superbly illustrated by the displayed psykter (wine cooler), *The Feasting Hetaerae* (23, A-111), decorated by the eminent late sixth-century B.C. painter Euphronios. His superb design still retains some features of the black-figure technique — the silhouette dominates, the figures are flat and the foreshortening is often distorted. It depicts four nude hetaerae, Akatha, Seklina, Smikra and Palaisto (their names are inscribed in purple), listening to music as they drink wine and play cottabus, a game of skill requiring the player to hit with a drop of wine a small dish mounted on a tripod. Next to the figure of Smikra is the legend reading: "To you I dedicate this drop, Leagros!" The virtuosity of the artist's draughtsmanship is here combined with his ability to harmonize the subject with the particular shape of the vessel. Of great artistic value are also many other Attic vessels, including the lecythi *Scene at a Tomb*, or *Man at a Stele* (19, A-118), *The Persian King Hunting* (20, A-115) and the well-known amphora *Comasts* (22, A-100).

Sculpture: 5th and 4th Centuries B.C.

Greek art reached its peak in the fifth century B.C. The items shown in Room 112, actually Roman copies of the Greek originals, were executed by the greatest sculptors of the classical epoch. Thus, the Campana Athena — thus named after Marquis da Campana, its previous owner — derives from Phidias' statue of Athena, while the basalt head of Doryphoros (*Spear-bearer*) is a copy of Polykleitos' original.

The sculptures in Room 114 are copies of late classical works of the fourth century B.C. Thus, the tragic overtones of the *Resting Heracles*, the furrowed forehead, the shadows about the eyes and the half-open, gasping mouth, are all characteristic of the illustrious Skopas, who was working at this period.

The Hermitage owns five Roman copies of Praxiteles' *Resting Satyr*. The soft-flowing modelling of the body that was typical of this great sculptor also distinguishes the Hermitage's torso of Aphrodite.

Several more copies in this same room give some idea of the art of Lysippos, the last of the great Classical masters. Among them are *Eros*

A

19, 20
21
22, 23

A

24

with a Bow, a head of Socrates and a relief portraying the orator Aeschines. Special note should be made of the small Roman copy of his *Heracles Slaying the Nemean Lion* (24, A-114) depicting the climax of the combat between man and beast; at first glance one senses the tremendous efforts of the combatants, but only by viewing the group from every side will one perceive the lion slowly choking in the mighty clutches of the mythological hero and realize that the beast is about to die. Sculpture to be viewed from different sides was an innovation and important achievement in fourth-century B.C. Greek art, heralding the ousting of the calm and static majesty of the previous century by the dynamism of movement.

Culture and Art of the Ancient Cities of the Northern Black Sea Coast

Many of the exhibits in the Hermitage Department of Classical Antiquities were unearthed along the northern Black Sea coast, where the

25

Greeks established colonies from the eighth century B.C. Without rupturing ties with metropolitan Greece, these colonies, either autonomous city-states or amalgamated into the Bosporan Kingdom, entered into lively contacts with the indigenous population — Scythians, Sindians, Meotians and other local tribes.

Phanagorian Figure Vessels

In 1869, splendid examples of fifth-century B.C. Attic pottery were discovered in what had apparently been a rich woman's burial, when excavations were undertaken of the necropolis at Phanagoria in the Taman peninsula. These were vessels for fragrances and ointments fashioned in the shape of painted figurines of Aphrodite (the goddess of love and beauty, who, according to the Greek myths, sprang from the foam of the sea, is depicted emerging from a seashell), of the legendary half-woman, half-bird Siren, and of the Sphinx (25, A-116), a winged monster who in

A

26—28

ancient Greece was represented as having the head and breasts of a woman and the body of a lion. Their vivid combination of painting and gilding discloses a certain affinity with both Greek statuary (whose original colour has, as a rule, not survived) and with small terra-cotta figurines.

Tanagra Terra-cottas

Although *terra-cotta* (baked clay) statuettes were made in many Greek cities and colonies in Asia Minor and along the Northern coast of the Black Sea, the most artistically precious and perfect were produced at Tanagra in Bœotian Greece. The Hermitage collection of such statuettes dating from the fourth and third centuries B.C. is among the world's best. Though many of their makers were influenced by Praxiteles' emphasis on lyricism and sensual earthly beauty, besides copying his celebrated statues, they also drew their subject matter from the life around them or adapted what they had seen, each in his own fashion, to harmonize with the medium, the different scale and the specific aspects of the technique employed.

The works shown in the exhibition, such as *Artemis* (26, A-121), *Aphrodite and Eros* (27, A-121) and *A Standing Woman* (28, A-121), confirm these characteristics.

The statuettes were cast in moulds and subsequently only in part modelled by hand, which allowed them to be made in great quantities. After drying and painting, the figurines were subjected to a short spell of firing. The Tanagra terra-cottas have become synonymous with elegance and the consummate perfection of form.

29

The Gonzaga Cameo (29, A-120)

Particularly remarkable amidst the wealth of engraved gems possessed
by the Hermitage, many of which are truly unique, is the celebrated
Gonzaga cameo, so called after the Gonzaga Dukes of Mantua in Italy,
who were its first European owners known to us. The gem, which was
cut in Alexandria in the third century B.C., depicts the Pharaoh Ptole-
my Philadelphus and his wife Arsinoë in completely idealized form,
without emphasizing their individual features. This type of double-
profile composition, with one face superimposed upon the other and the
contours of their silhouettes harmonized in such a way as to express
the unity and common identity of the subjects, subsequently enjoyed
great popularity. In this piece the unknown lapidary has shown a virtuoso handling of the three-layered sardonyx using the different texture
and colour of each layer to achieve a truly painterly effect.
The cameo's history is a rather chequered one. In 1630 invading Austrian forces seized the gem, hitherto in the possession of the Gonzagas,
the ruling house of Mantua. In 1648, the cameo, which by this time had
found its way to Prague, was captured by Swedish troops who presented it to Queen Christina in Stockholm; it returned to Italy, this time
to Rome, in 1654, when, after abdication, Christina entered a nunnery
there. After her death, it came into the possession of the Dukes of Odes-
calchi, from whom it was purchased by the Holy See in 1794. But just
two years later the French seized the gem and surrendered it to Em-

30, 31, 32
33, 34, 35
36, 37

A

press Josephine, who in 1814 presented it to the Russian Tsar Alexander I. Thus one of the world's finest and largest cameos — 15.7 by 11.8
centimeters — finally came to rest in the Hermitage.

The display includes many other notable carved gems engraved by the
masters of Ancient Greece, the Hellenistic world and Rome. These are
Zeus (31, A-120), one of the best cameos in the Hermitage collection,
the cameos *Dionysos* (30, A-120), *Venus with an Eagle* (32, A-120), *Lu-
cilla* (33, A-120), *Apollo and Artemis* (34, A-120), *Lucius Commodus* (35,
A-120), *Dionysos Riding a Chariot* (36, A-120) and *The Trial of Orestes*
(37, A-120).

39

The Tauride Venus (38, A-109)

Rightly ranked among the masterpieces of classical antiquity is the Hermitage statue of a nude Venus. Created by an anonymous sculptor in the third century B.C., it depicts the loveliest of the mythological goddesses as the ideal of perfect beauty. The sensual delightfulness of the shapes, set off by chaste restraint, imparts particular charm to the figure. The first antique sculpture to reach Russia, it was unearthed in Rome in 1718 and subsequently presented by Pope Clement XI to Peter the Great, who reciprocated with a gift of the relic of St. Bridget. In St. Petersburg it initially stood in the Summer Gardens, but was later moved to the Tauride Palace — whence its name.

Early Italian Art

Room 130, otherwise known as the Hall of Twenty Columns, is devoted to the art and culture of the colonies that the ancient Greeks set up in Italy in the seventh to second century B.C. Many artefacts illustrating the culture of Etruria, the most developed region of ancient Italy, were found in burial grounds and were related to the funerary cult. These include excellent examples of the so-called *bucchero* ware — vessels made of blackened fired clay and decorated with figurines, reliefs and engraved designs. Their shapes and black polished surfaces remind us of toreutic articles for which Etruria was famous.

Among the most remarkable artefacts made of bronze are the cinerary urn with a reclining figure of a youth, the head of a lion that was used to guard a burial chamber and the tripod stand with reliefs representing the Labours of Heracles.

Queen of Vases (39, A-130)

One of the best known Hermitage exhibits is a hydria, whose particular elegance has earned it the title of Regina Vasorum or Queen of Vases. The vessel was discovered in a fourth-century burial during excavations at ancient Cumae in Italy, its upright ribs are crossed by a horizontal band with representations of animals in relief. The main group, that of deities, is arranged on the shoulders of the vase where Demeter, the goddess of fertility, and her daughter Kore, are positioned centrally. By their side, in a chariot drawn by winged dragons, is the hero and demigod Triptolemus, sent by Demeter to instruct mankind in sowing. Also presented in relief are Dionysos, Aphrodite and other deities.

A

CULTURE AND ART OF ANCIENT ROME

Towards the end of the third century B.C. Rome dominated the whole territory of the Appenine peninsula. The power of the Roman state culminated in the first century B.C., when its domains extended over the vast territories of Europe, Asia and Africa. The reign of the first Roman Emperor, Octavian Augustus (30—14 B.C.), is considered the "golden age" in the history of Rome.

Statue of Octavian Augustus (40, A-127)

Of special note among sculptured monuments in the Roman collection of the Hermitage is the large marble statue of Emperor Octavian Augustus, one of those sculptures which had once decorated the various cities of the Empire symbolizing its power. The image of the Emperor is treated accordingly: the face is life-like yet somewhat idealized and the figure is given the posture of Zeus as depicted by Phidias in his famous statue for the temple at Olympia.

The exhibits demonstrate the main genres of Roman sculpture, notably temple, portrait and decorative statuary and carving in relief.

Portrait Sculpture

The best of the 120 examples of portrait sculpture in the Hermitage collection of ancient Roman art are portraits of Gaius Julius Caesar as a boy (41, A-127), Lucius Verus (42, A-107), Philip the Arab (43, A-107), a Syrian woman (44, A-107), Gnaeus Domitius Corbulo (45, A-127), a Roman man (46, A-127), Livia (47, A-127) and a youth (48, A-128).

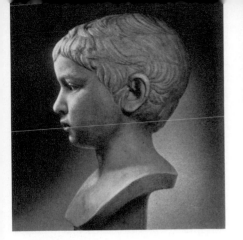

40
41, 42
43, 44

Lucius Verus, the co-ruler of Marcus Aurelius, is shown as an army
leader, with the image of the Gorgone Medusa on the breastplate and a
cloak flung over the shoulder. A formal state portrait as it is, the bust
gives, however, an extremely expressive evocation of the character. It
presents to us not only a man of power with a proud and haughty coun-
tenance but also a man paying much attention to his appearance.

Emperor Balbinus, in a third-century sculptured portrait, looks quite
different — as a man who ascended the throne by chance, at the desire
of the Senate and then, three months later, was killed like his prede-
cessor. The shrivelled, unshaven face of a weak-willed man with a per-
plexed look is evocative of his time — the period of the decline of Roman
power and the lack of stability in state affairs.

45, 46
47, 48 The bust of Philip the Arab is exceptional for its expressive realism.
The crudely done head, thick neck and massive shoulders endow the
portrait with a heavy magnificence emphasized by the dense folds of
the toga. However, a premonition of early death is already evident in
the anxious gaze and abrupt turn of the Emperor's head.

Roman portrait sculpture was without doubt an important phenomenon
in the history of world art. And while many valuable monuments of
antiquity were lost, nonetheless the barbarians did not destroy all of
Rome's masterpieces when putting the city to fire and sword. The great
heritage of classical antiquity served as a firm point of departure for
Europe's subsequent cultural advancement, a process that began in Renaissance Italy.

Western European Art

The early history of the Department of Western European Art may be said to resemble, in some respects, that of St. Petersburg — Leningrad itself. Just as the new Russian capital, founded on the barren, swampy banks of the Neva, came to rival the luxury and splendour of Europe's ancient capitals in a mere two and a half decades, so the collection of works of Western European art, which was started in 1764 — the date traditionally regarded as the year of the Hermitage's foundation — needed only twenty-five years to attain that wealth and variety which placed it on a par with the most celebrated collections of Western Europe.

Isolated specimens of Western European art had of course found their way into Russia during the preceding periods, especially during the reign of Peter the Great, but consistent and purposeful collecting began only in the second half of the eighteenth century. By the end of the century the Picture Gallery already contained about 2,500 canvases.

Now the Department holds over 7,500 paintings, 2,000 sculptural pieces, 500,000 drawings and engravings and some 67,000 objects of the applied arts. The exhibits are displayed in Rooms 200—308 on the first floor and in Rooms 314—50 on the second floor.

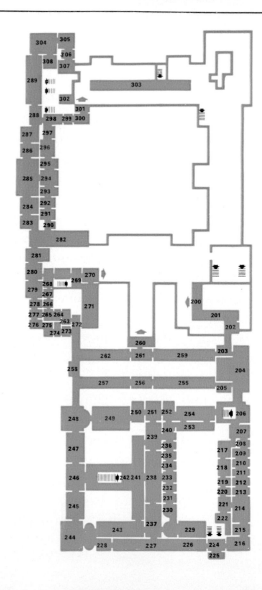

**First
floor**

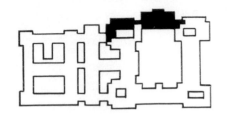

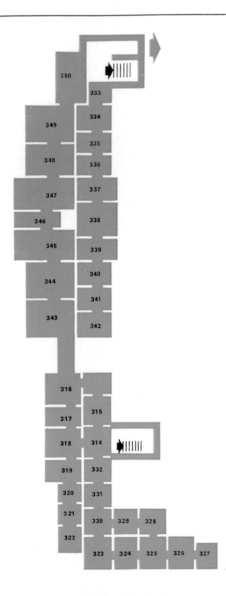

49

ITALIAN ART: 13th — 20th CENTURIES

To be found in this collection are many superb works by Renaissance and seventeenth- and eighteenth-century masters.

Simone Martini. *The Madonna from the Annunciation* (49, W-207)

Conspicuous among the work of proto-Renaissance masters is a small tempera panel by Simone Martini (*ca.* 1284—1344), actually the right-hand part of a diptych — the other half, depicting the Archangel Gabriel is in the National Gallery of Art in Washington. Though Gothic overtones are still pronounced, as is evidenced by the elongated proportions and two-dimensional treatment of the S-shaped figure and by the golden background, specific Renaissance characteristics are already manifest. Concrete human feeling is underlined; the Virgin is excited and taken aback by the unexpected news; her face is pensive and serious; her hand keeps her place in the partly open book that she has let fall on her lap. The soft-flowing lines of the figure and the gentle warm colour scheme produce a subtle harmony, emphasizing the intimacy of the scene, and generally evoking a sense of refined lyricism.

W

Filippino Lippi. *Adoration of*
the Infant Christ **(50, W-213)**

The tondo that Filippino Lippi (*ca.* 1457—1504) executed in tempera on
wood (it was subsequently transferred to a copper plate in the 1480s),
immediately catches the eye in the room devoted to fifteenth-century
painting. Whether it be the Madonna herself, bent over the Infant
Christ in reverent adoration, or the graceful angels in their semitranspar-
ent garments, all the figures radiate a subtle elegance; the artist is
rather concerned with the attainment of a definite cadence and mood
than with verisimilitude. The landscape in the background reveals a
knowledge of aerial perspective, though the picture largely conforms to
the norms of medieval art — a general characteristic of the Medici circle
to which Filippino Lippi belonged — as is reflected in the elongated
figures, differences in scale and various levels at which the figures are
positioned.

Despite the indubitable achievements of Filippino Lippi, however, it
was for the great masters of the period, notably Leonardo da Vinci,
Raphael, Michelangelo, Giorgione and Titian, to play the decisive role
in establishing the new art of the High Renaissance.

W

51

Leonardo da Vinci. *Madonna with a Flower*
(The Benois Madonna) **(51, W-214)**

This picture, which Leonardo da Vinci (1452—1519) painted in 1478 in
Florence, where he began his artistic career, already reveals the great
master's mature hand and original talent. The heart of the painting's
meaning is expressed in the centre of the composition, with the child
stretching out towards the flower and examining this new object, while
the young mother attentively watches her baby, delighting in its awak-
ening consciousness. In fact, it is rather the idea of cognition of the
surrounding world, and the profound meaning of motherhood than the
telling of a story or the ordinary glimpse of life so characteristic of
Leonardo's quattrocento predecessors that lie at the roots of this remarkable picture.

Renouncing the Madonna's traditional central position and shifting her
figure slightly to the left, Leonardo thus makes the composition more
natural and free. He restores balance by introducing a window on the
right. Besides the sources of light from front left and top, usual for that
period, here light is also coming from the window in the depths of the
painting, which has enabled the artist to convey the impression of space

within the interior. Further, not only the Madonna's appearance — she is dressed like the women of Leonardo's time and has a contemporary, fashionable hair-style — but also, primarily, a profound knowledge of the human anatomy, physiognomy, the proportions of the child's body and so on, have combined to impart a hitherto unprecedented penetration and vividness to this traditional motif.

Leonardo da Vinci. *Madonna and Child*
(The Litta Madonna) **(52, W-214)**

Painted evidently in Milan, where Leonardo moved in 1482, this picture reveals a terse compositional arrangement with symmetrically disposed windows. Against the dark background of a wall, the figures, illuminated from a frontal source and modelled in subtle chiaroscuro, seem to assume a three-dimensional quality. The eye is caught by the centrally positioned crimson of the Madonna's dress. Though her face is turned almost in profile and the eyelids are lowered, one clearly senses the warm, tender glance of maternal love turned towards the Infant Christ. The Child's eyes too are extremely expressive. These two very concrete, yet meaningful, images reflect the humanistic ideals of the perfection

W

53

of man and the harmony of the entire Universe. It is precisely such works by the great Leonardo that marked the first assertion of the style of the High Renaissance in Italy.

Raphael. *The Conestabile Madonna* (53, W-229)

In this masterpiece, which Raphael (1483—1520) painted in 1502—3, harmony, tranquillity and the human being's unity with nature are extolled with a profound lyricism and spontaneity. Indeed the peacefully pensive look of a certain sadness on the face of the youthful Madonna is truly consonant with the mood that emanates from the spring landscape with its green meadows, solitary trees on the river bank and the distant chain of snow-capped mountains. The flowing lines of the figures that agree so well with the picture's round shape, the soft muted tints and the setting with its airy, limpid distances, all serve to accentuate to a still greater degree the fragile daintiness of this poetic characterization of a young mother and the beauty of the world around her.

54

The Hermitage's other Raphael, *The Holy Family* or *Madonna with the Beardless St. Joseph* (54, W-229), which was painted in 1506, demonstrates the painter's consummate mastery in creating ideal and elevated images, yet without destroying the impression of ease and convincingness, and also indicates the new approaches he evolved in his effort to achieve a well-integrated composition.

Majolica and Furniture

The humanitarian essence of Renaissance culture also marks the Italian applied art of the period, whose basic feature was a constructive

W

55
56
57, 58

clarity of form, but with each object's designated purpose always in view. Of special note in the rich collection of Italian majolica, of which up to 500 examples are exhibited, are works by the craftsmen of the four major centres of Faenza, Urbino, Deruta and Castel Durante.

Thus, Faenza majolica is celebrated for its overglaze decoration with a predominantly white-and-yellow design over the light blue pigment fused with the tin glaze (56, W-229). Urbino, which after 1525 took the lead in majolica manufacture and which influenced artists throughout almost the whole of Italy, was noted for its Istoriato style — wares decorated with historical, mythical, biblical or genre scenes, or images from the fine arts or literature. Of interest among Urbino wares in the Hermitage is a wine-cooler (55, W-229). Another significant majolica centre was Deruta, whose produce was notable for its simple and monumental forms and also for the use of lustre, a pigment imparting an iridescent metallic sheen that enhances the overall decorative effect. The wedding dish (57, W-229) and the vase (58, W-229) are two remarkable products of Castel Durante.

Extensively displayed, not only in the room, where the majolica wares (59, W-229) are exhibited but also in other rooms devoted to Italian art, is a collection of artistically embellished furniture, for example *cassoni*, marriage chests, with beautiful carved, gilded and inlaid decoration that not infrequently were the work of famed Italian artists.

60

Michelangelo. *The Crouching Boy* (60, W-230)

The Crouching Boy is the only work of the great sculptor, painter and architect Michelangelo Buonarotti (1475—1564) in the Soviet Union. Even in this small piece, carved during the 1520s—1530s, the power and monumental talent of its creator can be sensed. The resilient bent figure, treated in a generalized manner, personifies an indomitable will and unyielding force.

Although originally intended as a decoration for a tomb of the ruling Medici family in Florence, it was not incorporated in the final version.

Giorgione. *Madonna and Child in a Landscape* (61, W-218)

The first to bring the High Renaissance to Venice was Giorgione da Castelfranco (1478—1510).

Painted around 1504, this picture is largely a quattrocento piece, the figures being insufficiently well integrated with the background landscape, the Infant's movements constrained, and the folds of the clothing stiff and excessively complex, especially in the Madonna's lap. At the

61

same time it is clearly a typical Giorgione in respect of its pensive mood, emotion-charged landscape and wealth of colour.

Giorgione. *Judith* (62, W-217)

This painting is one of the few absolutely authenticated works of Giorgione. It illustrates the biblical story of Judith, who, when the Assyrians laid seige to her native town ventured into the tent of the enemy general Holofernes and, staying with him after a feast, seized the opportunity to decapitate him while he slept, thus compelling the enemy to withdraw. The basic message is one of undertaking a heroic deed to achieve liberation, yet Giorgione, a distinctly lyrical painter, has endowed his picture with a characteristically poetic note. The emphasis is placed on the softly modelled silhouette of the figure; the colour scheme is remarkable for its exquisite blend of cerulean blue and wine red, united by a shade of lilac. Giorgione reveals a virtuoso hand in the use of barely perceptible tonal values and subtle gradations of colour to convey varying lighting effects.

W

62

Titian. *Danaë* **(63, W-221)**

Titian (1475/90—1576), the greatest of the Venetian masters, is represented in the Hermitage by eight pictures.
The legend of Danaë was no doubt one of Titian's favourite subjects, as
he painted five pictures on this theme. As the story goes, King Acrisius,
to forestall an oracle that predicted his death at the hand of the son
of his daughter Danaë, confined her in a tower to prevent her ever mar-
rying. However, Zeus, hearing of her loveliness, visited her in the form

of a shower of gold. In the Hermitage picture, painted between 1546 and 1553, Danaë — like other mythological heroines in similar paintings, which Titian himself termed *poesies* — is given the seductively rounded forms of a Venetian lady. Yet the superbly represented nude female figure, though sensual, is at the same time the noble epitome of beauty.

Titian. *The Penitent Magdalene* (64, W-221)

In this masterpiece, painted in the 1560s, the artist again extols the beauties of the female body; however there can already be sensed a mood of anxiety, occasioned by premonitions of the coming crisis of humanism.

With Titian, unlike Leonardo and Raphael, who were more preoccupied with linear and chiaroscuro modelling, colour was of the utmost importance; form, dimensions and texture are conveyed through the use of diverse colour combinations; at times the line seems totally absent, as for instance in the way a vessel is depicted, even though the article itself is undeniably concrete and real.

Titian. *St. Sebastian* (65, W-221)

By the 1570s the artist, hitherto one of the most joyous of Renaissance masters, tragically realized that the humanitarian ideal was an unattainable illusion and began to create images of great dramatic force. St. Sebastian, put to death by the enemies of his Christian faith, is seen as a martyr of indomitable spirit, yet a solitary figure in a dark and

hostile world. Not only does the colour scheme, which rests on contrasting dark and violet-yellow tones, sustains the atmosphere of gloom and tragedy, but the vigorous use of finger and spatula in place of brush to dab on the paint, also serves to heighten the expressiveness of this profound work.

Caravaggio. *The Lute Player* (66, W-237)

A true masterpiece, though an early work, this is the only picture by Caravaggio (1571—1610), an artist of the Roman school, that the Hermitage has in its possession. Created about 1595, when the painter was

W

66

still at the beginning of his artistic career, it nonetheless already reflects many characteristic features of Caravaggio's unique talent. Numerous novel approaches were devised to emphasize the palpable quality of the material world. The figure and the various objects around are presented in close-up, using a side lighting emanating from an unseen source, while the dark background imparts a three-dimensional clarity. The finger-board of the instrument is pointed straight at the viewer to generate an impression of its solidity and to accentuate the space in front of its player; the violin has been placed slantwise across the table and the bow leant against the violin at an angle to it, so that its shadow, falling on the table, again creates the illusion of space. Despite the everyday nature of the genre scene, the picture possesses a monumental quality.

It should be noted that many of the techniques that Caravaggio invented were subsequently borrowed, at times merely for the sake of form, by his followers in many countries of Western Europe; the Hermitage boasts a widely representative collection of works by Caravaggio's followers and imitators.

The Bologna Academy

The work of the two brothers, Annibale and Agostino Carracci, and their cousin Ludovico Carraci, who together established the Bologna

67

Academy of Fine Arts, one of the first in Europe, reveals a desire to canonize the achievements of the Renaissance masters and establish eternal norms of beauty. As a result the life-like quality of representation was often sacrificed in favour of the falsely conceived notions of beauty and grandeur.

The Holy Women at the Sepulchre which Annibale Carracci (1560—1609) painted in the 1590s, though distinguished by its compositional clarity, portrays completely static figures, totally devoid of individual characteristics, dressed in stylized "antique" robes and given to theatrical gesture. However, his self-portrait of the same period displays a much freer style of painting, demonstrating the artist's faculty for keen observation and fine realist talent, that came into play when he neglected the tenets of purely academic art.

Sculptures by Bernini

Gian Lorenzo Bernini (1598—1680), the greatest exponent of the Baroque style in sculpture, is represented by several works, outstanding among which is his terracotta *Self-portrait* (67, W-232); a piece full of inspired grandeur and inner power. The play of light and shade on the deeply furrowed face, topped by an unruly shock of hair, enhances the expressiveness of the picture emphasizing the energy of the man of action. Unconstrained by the tastes of a client, the sculptor has portrayed himself without idealization, not attempting to conceal his old age and

W

68

without ostentation in dress and accessories. Also of great artistic value
are his *bozzetti*, that is, small moulded studies for his larger well-
known works.

Executed in terra-cotta and vividly conveying to us the artist's original
conception, they introduce the viewer to his searches which resulted in
the creation of such famous works as the sculptural group *The Ecstasy
of St. Theresa* in the Cornaro Chapel of S. Maria della Vittoria in Rome.
The Hermitage study for this group (68, W-232) has reached us somewhat damaged.

Bernini had a tremendous influence on many seventeenth- and eighteenth-century sculptors, including Antonio Canova (1757—1822), whose
work is extensively exhibited in the Gallery of the History of Ancient
Painting (Room 241). There are some fifteen sculptures by Canova,
including *Cupid and Psyche*, *Hebe*, *Paris* and *The Kiss of Cupid*. One of
Canova's most renowned works is *The Three Graces* (69, W-241).

70

In eighteenth-century Italian art pride of place was taken by the Venetian school to which belonged the great master of decorative painting
Giovanni Battista Tiepolo (1696—1770), and the leading painters of
vedutas, such as Antonio Canaletto (1697—1768), Francesco Guardi
(1712—1793) and Bernardo Bellotto (1720—1780).

Tiepolo. *The Triumph of the Emperor* (70, W-238)

Intended for the decoration of the Dolfino Palace in Venice, this huge
piece represents the return of the Emperor and his legions after a vic-

71

torious campaign, as an event that had really taken place. Tiepolo revealed a profound knowledge of the very special precepts of decorative painting allowing for the need to adorn large expanses of wall, harmonize with sumptuous palace décor and have the paintings viewed from a distance. The elongated proportions of the topmost figures assume a convincing reality when seen from below, as the entire composition is designed with a particular angle of view in mind, which also explains the absence of detail. The mood of uplift and pomp is emphasized by the artist's sweeping manner and vibrant use of colour.

W

72

The brilliant achievements of the art of townscape are illustrated in the Hermitage by the works of Canaletto's pupils, Francesco Guardi and Bernardo Bellotto.

Although the sky occupies a very small part of the canvas in Guardi's *View of a Square with a Palace* (71, W-235), it is saturated with light and air. The spectator's gaze is attracted towards the depth of the picture where the brightly-lit palace is seen behind the dark arch. The people are represented in movement, either walking away to the back of the courtyard or approaching the viewer, a device which also serves to enhance the effect of space. Outlined in a flowing sketchy manner, the figures seem to be moving in a lively, animated atmosphere.

Among works by twentieth-century Italian painters pictures by Giorgio Morandi (1890—1964) and Renato Guttuso (born 1912) occupy a prominent place.

Morandi. *Still Life* (72, W-337)

In this poetic canvas the artist places emphasis on the interaction of objects and seeks to achieve a harmonious composition based on the carefully thought-out rhythm of the whole. The objects painted in bright hues are enveloped in vibrant air and appear remarkably lucid.

73

Guttuso. *Rocco and His Son* **(73, W-337)**

This picture is one of the artist's best in the Hermitage collection. It is
painted in his characteristic expressive manner marked by a dynamic
linear design, generalized modelling of form and sharp contrasts of colour. The work is pervaded with a sense of tragedy reflecting the contradictions of the contemporary world; but although the painting ex-
presses a deep anxiety, it evokes at the same time a feeling of warmth
and hope.

W

74

SPANISH ART: 15th — EARLY 19th CENTURIES

The Hermitage has one of the world's finest collections of Spanish painting, with all the great masters such as El Greco, Ribera, Zurbarán, Velázquez, Murillo and Goya represented in Rooms 239 and 240.

El Greco. *The Apostles Peter and Paul* (74, W-240)

El Greco (1541—1614) was one of the first Spanish artists to portray the two apostles together. Yet his sympathies clearly lie with St. Paul, who, according to legend, converted to Christianity the painter's native Greek island of Crete. However, though the two apostles are somewhat opposite in characterization, there is no direct contrasting. St. Paul is presented as a meditative person who is by no means a zealot; the portrayal of St. Peter, with his meek eyes and suppliant gesture, is also a probing psychological study. *The Apostles Peter and Paul* relates of earthly conflicts and spiritual values as variously evinced in human nature.

Ribera. *St. Jerome Listening to the Sound of the Trumpet* (75, W-239)

José Ribera (1591—1652) was for a long time attached to the court of the Spanish viceroy in Naples, and the influence of Caravaggio is evident in much of his work, as for instance in *St. Jerome Listening to the Sound of the Trumpet* and *St. Sebastian and St. Irene*, both of which are on view at the Hermitage.

St. Jerome is traditionally depicted either in his cell — a Doctor of the Church, he produced the Latin translation of the Bible, known as "The Vulgate" — or as a hermit; Ribera took this latter variation for the subject of the Hermitage picture which he painted in his youth in 1626. St. Jerome is shown listening to the sound of the trumpet heralding Doomsday. The abruptly turning figure, the exaggerated, *tenebroso* contrast of light and shade, and the generally characteristic desire of Spanish painters to portray saints in monumental proportions — here the low horizon seems to elevate the figure — highlight the dramatic significance of the event. Ribera, the first great master of Spanish realist painting, pays close attention to the actual features, drawn from nature, and convincingly portrays an old man's body.

W

76

Zurbarán. *St. Lawrence* (76, W-239)

Francisco de Zurbarán (1598—1664) painted this picture, the best of his works in the possession of the Hermitage, for the Monastery of St. Joseph in Seville.

This painting belongs to the flourishing period of the artist's career. The portrayal of a solitary saint was common in Spanish art at that time. Martyrs were depicted, as a rule, with the instrument that had been used to torture them. In this case, the saint, the first deacon of Rome, is shown with his traditional symbol, the gridiron, as he was put to death by roasting on the grid.

The face is a portrait study of an actual monk, the clothing is presented in scrupulous detail, and the figure of the saint is monumentally sculptural — most likely the influence of Zurbarán's teacher, a painter of sculptured devotional images. Sturdy, firm of foot and simple of face, the saint, who is depicted clasping a massive iron grid, radiates courage and significance.

Velázquez. *Portrait of Count Olivarez* (77, W-239)

Count Olivarez was one of the few persons outside of the royal family whom Spain's greatest painter of the seventeenth century, Diego Rodriguez de Silva y Velázquez (1599—1660), portrayed several times. Though the all-powerful favourite, who actually ruled the country in place of its weak monarch, was the painter's good friend remaining so even after his downfall, Velázquez has by no means prettified his sitter in this portrait, painted about 1640. Behind the smile and gentle outer calm, one discerns this adventurer's perceptive mind and iron will. The face is moulded with a virtuoso hand; by modifying the direction and character of his brushwork the artist has conveyed with supreme skill the smoothness of the hair, the bushiness of the whiskers, the bluish tinge of the close-shaven outward thrusting chin, and the moist sheen of the eyes which seem to be examining the viewer attentively. The picture's laconic, black-dominated palette is characteristic of the painter's coloristic gift.

78

Velázquez. *Luncheon* **(78, W-239)**

At a time when many in Spain preferred religious painting to the genre, Velázquez often and willingly applied his brush to what was contemptuously termed as the *bodegón* — from the Spanish word for 'tavern'. In *Luncheon* which was painted around 1617/18, he depicts three hidalgoes at a meal. The two on the left are taken from life and can be seen in some other paintings by the artist, while the young man on the right is apparently the painter himself. Velázquez, who was only some eighteen years old at the time, skilfully arranges his clear-cut composition. By means of the well-lit flatness of the white table-cloth he has been able to cleverly dispose and integrate the three figures, while the sharply contrasting play of light and shade has served to impart a tangibility to the objects depicted. The arrangement of the objects on the table, all placed in isolation from one another and thereby attracting individual attention, is particularly characteristic of the Spanish still life at the time of its flourishing.

79

Murillo. *Boy with a Dog* (79, W-239)

Bartolomé Esteban Murillo (1617—1682) was extremely fond of portraying children, whom, however, he tended to idealize in his later years, thus at times imparting a note of sentimentality to his paintings. The Hermitage's *Boy with a Dog* was produced in the 1650s, and ranks among the best Murillos of this type; their prime merit lies in their freshness and truth to life. The painter's ability to present a seemingly chance posture and convey atmospheric effects in the landscape, subsequently attracted the attention of the Impressionists.

A companion piece, *Girl Fruit-seller*, is in the Pushkin Museum of Fine Arts, Moscow.

Murillo. *The Immaculate Conception* (80, W-239)

The Immaculate Conception, a theme popular with Spanish painters of the seventeenth century, was one to which Murillo also often turned his hand. The canonical presentation was to have the Virgin clothed in a

W

blue gown and white cape, standing in a halo of sunshine with feet on the moon and with twelve stars above. The Budapest Murillo is precisely of this kind. However, the Hermitage version, which was painted later, has the Assumption motif as its keynote — hence the picture's other title, *The Assumption of the Madonna*, used by some scholars. The Virgin has her eyes and hand turned upwards, her cape streams out behind her, the angels, too, soar upwards, and, finally, the lower, darker portion of the painting yields to a progressively increasing brightness as it approaches the sky — all this combining to create the impression of ascent.

81

Goya. *Portrait of the Actress*
Antonia Zárate (81, W-239)

The world of the theatre was familiar to Francisco Goya (1746—1828),
who time and again painted actors. He twice portrayed the actress Antonia Zárate (the other version is in Ireland), but not on the stage, as
what evidently attracted him was her charm rather than her acting; he
underlies the subtlety and depth of her character, and especially her
tragic destiny (separated from her husband, she died of consumption
at the age of thirty-six, shortly after the Hermitage portrait was completed in 1811). What holds attention most in this small intimate piece are
the eyes, in which an inner anxiety is concealed behind an outer calm.
With his virtuoso hand and characteristic ease has Goya painted the
headdress and the transparent scarf which is draped across the sitter's
breast in energetic folds.

WESTERN EUROPEAN ARMS AND ARMOUR:
15th — 17th CENTURIES (82, W-243)

The display mounted in Room 243 shows only a fraction of the Hermitage's highly representative collection of some 8,000 items of Western European arms and armour, the nucleus of which consists of the collections transferred in 1895 from the Tsarskoye Selo Arsenal, Virtually all types of arms and armour used from the fifteenth to seventeenth century are represented, from the simplest of bludgeons and maces to muskets and ceremonial halberds, and from suits of mail for the foot soldier to the highly decorative armour worn by mounted knights when jousting at tournaments. The diverse techniques employed to ornament arms and armour range from blueing, tempering and gilding to engraving, embossing and etching, as well as inlaying with ivory, horn and other valuable materials. Best represented, with pieces of the highest quality on display, are the arms and armour of Germany.

NETHERLANDISH ART: 15th — EARLY 17th CENTURIES

The Low Countries, otherwise known as the Netherlands, had already been economically well developed, thanks to the advance of industry and commerce, by the thirteenth — fourteenth centuries, while the process of political unification commenced in the next, fifteenth century. Concurrently, local Renaissance art sought to mirror life more fully.

Campin. *The Holy Trinity* and *The Virgin and Child*. Diptych (83, W-261)

W

An outstanding exponent of the art of the Low Countries over the 1420s and 1430s was Robert Campin (1378/79—1444).

The composition of *The Holy Trinity* panel is still of a largely traditional order, with its three-dimensional modelling of the figures and the introduction of a pedestal indicative of Gothic sculptural influences. The Holy Trinity — the three Persons of the Godhead, i.e. God the Father, God the Son and God the Holy Ghost — are presented in stiffened, static postures against a neutral background without depth. Also reminiscent of sculpture are the small figures on the throne — the pelican feeding its young with its own blood, emblematic of Christ's sacrifice, the Eucharist, and the lioness, symbolizing the belief that the cubs are born dead and remain so for three days until the lion, a symbol of the Resurrection, roars and breathes life into them. Such religious symbolism was characteristic of art in the fifteenth century.

However, in the other panel, depicting the Virgin and Child, Campin has almost completely broken with the Gothic tradition. The Virgin, who is portrayed shielding the Infant with her hand from the heat of the flames in the fireplace, is presented in a room in an ordinary Netherlands house, with all its furnishings faithfully reproduced in full detail — even down to the heads of the nails in the wooden shutters. The washbasin and jug on the small washstand, together with the towel draped over the rail nearby, symbolizing the Virgin's purity and innocence as they do, are, however, painted so life-like that they are often taken to be no more than ordinary household articles. Finally, a landscape is to be glimpsed through the window.

In Netherlandish art the characteristically Renaissance interest in the real world was reflected by an empirical approach unlike that of the Italians, for example, with their learned and theoretical argumentation. However, though Netherlandish painters were ignorant of the laws of perspective, with, for instance, floors steeply inclined in such a manner that the figures on them seem to be slipping down towards the lower edge of the picture, and though Campin, for one, depicts his jug, basin and washstand from different angles, nonetheless they were ahead of their Italian counterparts in techniques and technology, and by the use of oils on white priming managed to impart to colour an intense vibrancy and glow.

W

83

One of Campin's pupils was the illustrious artist Rogier van der Weyden (*ca.* 1399—1464).

Van der Weyden. *St. Luke Painting the Virgin* (84, W-262)

According to medieval legend, St. Luke the Evangelist painted the first pictures of the Virgin. Though the subject of this picture is the Virgin and Child posing for St. Luke, it is not the religious aspect that dominates its imagery. Rather it is a typically Renaissance work with its interest in the human being and desire to convey the reality of the surrounding world. The figures are set not within an enclosed space as in medieval art but against the background of a sweeping and receding cityscape, reproducing with almost documentary authenticity the old buildings of Brussels. One more innovation is the representation of the spiritual state of man. Van der Weyden depicted St. Luke — who may possibly be the artist's self-portrait — in a pose of meditative concentration and reverent awe for his sitter. Unlike the Italian masters, the Netherlandish artist pays equal attention to the people he portrays and to the various details of the setting. But though garments and jewellery

are conveyed with scrupulous skill, at the same time a certain degree of constraint is sensed, with, for example, the folds of clothing so excessively elaborate that at times it is hard to imagine the movements of the body that they conceal; furthermore the figure of the Infant is too long and rigid, and the forefront seems isolated from the background.

The story of how this diptych was acquired by the Hermitage is a rather curious one. In 1850 a portrait of St. Luke was purchased for the Hermitage at the Hague. Then, thirty-four years later, another picture, this time of the Virgin and Child, which was believed to be by another artist, was acquired. Hermitage experts discovered that the two paintings were the two wings of Weyden's well-known work, and it was decided to transfer them from their wooden panels to canvas. Close scrutiny will reveal the vertical line of connection running along the centre of the picture, of which the right-hand half is slightly darker.

The next, sixteenth century saw the flourishing of art in the Low Countries. In this period such new, individual kinds of painting as the genre scene, landscape and still life appeared.

85

Dirck Jacobsz. Group Portraits

The sixteenth century also saw the emergence of an interest in group portraits, subsequently extremely popular, especially in the Northern Netherlands. Most remained in the hands of the guilds or companies that commissioned them, and are thus still in the Netherlands now. All the more remarkable, therefore, are the two Hermitage group portraits of companies of Amsterdam archers and musketeers, that were executed by Dirck Jacobsz (*ca.* 1497—1567), one of the founders of this kind of painting.

Lucas van Leyden. *The Healing of the Blind Man of Jericho* (85, W-262)

In this piece Lucas van Leyden (1489/94—1533) depicts a scene from the Gospels which tells how Jesus restored the sight of a blind man beside the walls of Jericho, which the blast of trumpets had brought to the ground. The protagonists have been skilfully positioned centrally, in the Italianate manner, at a distance from the crowd. However, the essence of the painting is not so much the miracle, as the response it evokes. All eyes are turned and all hands point to where the miraculous healing has taken place. On the whole this is a genre scene with figures dressed in the national costumes worn in the painter's lifetime and with a varied, vivid colour scheme — clearly indicative of the Netherlandish artistic tradition.

FLEMISH ART: 17th CENTURY

The resistance movement waged in the Low Countries throughout the sixteenth century against the alien yoke and feudal system culminated, at the start of the following, seventeenth, century, in the emergence of the independent bourgeois Dutch Republic in the north. Though the southern provinces, the largest of which was Flanders, still remained in the hands of the Spanish crown, the revolutionary struggles brought in their wake the cultural uplift responsible for the flowering of seventeenth-century Flemish art, which was marked by the appearance of such eminent masters as Rubens, Van Dyck, Jordaens and Snyders.

W

The excellent collection in the possession of the Hermitage includes some forty works by Peter Paul Rubens (1577—1640), the leading artist of the Flemish school of painting.

In the monumental canvases he produced for the decoration of palaces and Catholic churches he tended to emphasize the heroism of the noble deed and extol the free and good man; a passive attitude to life was deeply foreign to Rubens.

Rubens. *Christ in the House of Simon* (86, W-247)

The drama of this picture, based on a story from the Gospels, revolves around the conflict between faith and faithlessness. Simon the Pharisee and his adherents furiously rebuke Christ for having allowed Mary Magdalene to wash his feet and for saying: "Wherefore, I say unto thee, Her sins, which are many, are forgiven." "Who is this that forgiveth sins also?" they shout, showing that they stand in complete opposition to Christ and his disciples — as underlined by the picture's left-to-right movement towards the figure of Christ. In the execution of this piece Rubens was assisted by his pupils: the Apostle Peter was painted by Van Dyck, the girl in the upper part of the canvas by Jordaens, and the dog most likely by Snyders.

Rubens. *Perseus and Andromeda* (87, W-247)

This picture, one of Rubens' best on a theme borrowed from classical mythology, was painted in the 1620s when the artist was at the height of his powers. It strikingly reveals the very special nature of the style Rubens established, that of Flemish Baroque — evinced both in the way he conveyed the national features of his characters and also in his very concept of ideal beauty, in his interpretation of the Flemish dream of a strong-willed and energetic advocate of justice. This time, the artist, who in other pictures frequently portrayed scenes of dynamic intensity, has preferred to present not the high point of the story, when Perseus battles with the monster to save the lovely Andromeda, but rather the hero's eventual triumph — albeit at a moment when the fury of the passions kindled by the duel have still not fully subsided.

W

86
87

86
87

Perseus, in his gleaming dark armour and swirling scarlet cloak is depicted in a forward thrusting posture; above, the Goddess of Glory
descends from the skies to crown the victor; meanwhile his handsome
steed, Pegasus, has spread its mighty wings. Rubens has deliberately
exaggerated the hero's brawny legs to stress his vigour, temperament
and physical strength, and to contrast him to the nude, glowing body
of Andromeda upon which the pink, yellow and blue of surrounding
objects are reflected. The shadows are limpid and her body seems surrounded by air, illuminated by a gentle light. Perseus is captivated by
the ethereal beauty of Andromeda, whose love rewards him for his gallant deed. The winning of prosperity and liberty by heroic effort and
struggle is the optimistic message, one which was fully consonant with
the mood of Rubens' compatriots.

Rubens. *The Coronation of Marie de' Medici* (88, W-247)

Occupying a significant place in the Hermitage collection are the
sketches that Rubens made for a large cycle devoted to Marie de' Medici, sketches for structures that were to decorate Antwerp upon the ar-
rival of the Spanish King Ferdinand's new viceroy, or for such individual works as, for example, the *Lion Hunt*. In 1621—25 this "king of
painters and painter of kings" created a series of pictures intended for
decorating the Luxembourg Palace. Devoted to the life of Marie de' Medici, Queen of France, these allegorical pieces portray the gods and
other personages of the ancient myths. Only one can truly be termed a
history painting, namely the magnificent sketch for *The Coronation of
Marie de' Medici*, depicting the ceremony in the Paris Cathedral of
St. Denis, where, in great pomp and in the presence of King Henri IV

89

and his court, on 13 May 1610, Cardinal François de Joyeuse placed the crown of France on the head of the Italian Duchess Marie de' Medici. By means of dynamic, seemingly careless brushstrokes Rubens has outlined with unerring accuracy all the basic elements of the future canvas — its composition, colour scheme and lighting effects.

Rubens. *Portrait of a Lady in Waiting* (89, W-247)

The talent of Rubens as a portrait painter has been clearly revealed in the likeness of a lady in waiting to the Infanta Isabella, the ruler of the Netherlands. The lady in waiting is represented in such a way that the viewer's attention is focused on her face. The austere sharp outlines

90

of her dark dress and the pattern of dense folds of her lace collar serve to accentuate the softness and tenderness of the young girl's poetic image.

Rubens. *Bacchus* (90, W-247)

This picture, one of Rubens's best achievements, was painted towards the end of his life. Resorting to hyperbole, the great Flemish master has depicted the ancient Roman god of wine and revelry not as a slim and handsome youth, as earlier artists so frequently did, but as a massive, fat-bellied toper, the apotheosis of human flesh, that, bathed in an ethereal luminous glow, seems the very incarnation of nature itself.

87

W

91

Van Dyck. *A Family Group* (91, W-246)

Anthony van Dyck (1599—1641) is represented at the Hermitage by twenty-six paintings, which illustrate every stage of his career.

This picture, one of Van Dyck's finest early works painted in Antwerp, was done *alla prima*, with light dabs of almost dry pigments, the particles of which, along with the partly untouched grain of the canvas, serve to produce a live shimmering surface. The straightforward and natural character of the relationship between the persons portrayed and the viewer is most appealing; thus one seems to physically feel the attentive and calm gaze of the wife, while the husband seems to be addressing the viewer and expecting a reply. The immediacy of this rapport was an innovation subsequently borrowed by many artists.

92

Van Dyck. *Portrait of Sir Thomas Chaloner* (92, W-246)

The portrait of Sir Thomas Chaloner (one of the men who signed the order for the beheading of King Charles I, for which he was banished after the Restoration), a masterly and extremely life-like work, was executed by the artist himself — though, like Rubens, he often drew upon the assistance of his pupils. Almost in the nature of a sketch, with its light brushwork directly on the thick white priming, the technique of the portrait has considerably added to the impression of liveliness generated by the face of this man, although he is already past the prime of life. Masterpieces like this, which are of Van Dyck's later period, refute the opinion that he supposedly gradually abandoned his true-to-life approach in favour of a formal idealization.

93

Ceremonial Portraits by Van Dyck

Several pictures in the Hermitage collection relate to Van Dyck's later years. In his large dress portraits of King Charles I, queen consort Henrietta Maria, and the courtiers Thomas Wharton and the Earl of Danby, the artist has blended a virtuoso treatment of uniquely characteristic facial features with a tendency to exalt the sitter and highlight his or her social standing. This effect was achieved by emphasizing the richness of the garments and the appropriate choice of other accessories, as well as by the vertically arranged composition and the elongated proportions designed to be seen from below and thus enhancing the impression of elegance and majesty.

Jordaens. *The Bean King* (93, W-245)

Among the several Hermitage pictures by Jacob Jordaens (1593—1678), best known is his portrayal of the festivities attending Twelfth Night, the Feast of the Epiphany. According to tradition, that person who found in his slice of pie the bean specially placed there in advance was acclaimed the Bean King, to whose health all the other revellers drank. In all his variations on this theme the artist prefers to introduce heroic types, and to interpret motifs taken from life with an air of generalized uplift. The three-dimensional nature of the group in the foreground has been particularly stressed. Indeed, a fondness for scenes filled with people and things shown in close-up is characteristic of the artist.

Snyders. *Still Lifes*

At a time when most Flemish painters were trying their hands at different subjects, Frans Snyders (1579—1657) remained faithful to the still life. The underlying message of his pastries and stalls piled with fish, fowl, fruit and vegetables, was the exaltation of the earth's fertility, the richness of nature. He gave a virtuoso treatment to nature's bounties, preferring, however, to let his pupils paint in people wherever required to add an entertaining, narrative element to the picture, as he found the portrayal of human beings of less interest. The large cycle of highly decorative pieces of similar composition and format that he painted for the Bishop of Bruges was executed in the grand manner of Rubens and extol the fullness, beauty and diversity of life. An illustrative example is *A Fish Shop* (94, W-245).

Brouwer. *Peasant in a Tavern* (95, W-245)

When starting out as painter, Adriaen Brouwer (1606—1638) often depicted peasants; later he turned to urban outcasts, waits and vagabonds, all to reveal an unprepossessing side of life, which other Flemish artists ignored. In his best Hermitage piece, *Peasant in a Tavern*, he has portrayed a derelict with keen perceptiveness and potent realism. Aptly represented are his posture, sluggish movement, heavy-hanging head and bloated, besotted face with the narrow slits of its puffy eyes. His drinking companion's mocking and crooked grin imparts a mood of ironic bitterness. A first-rate colourist, Brouwer with great tact and taste contrasts the faded bluish green of the clothes with the pink of the old man's face and the wine-pink of the glass, against the dark background.

95

Teniers. *Kermess* (96, W-245)

In the work he did in many branches of painting, David Teniers the Younger (1610—1690) portrayed scenes taken from surrounding life, seeking, however, to highlight the comical aspect of reality and avoid acute characterization. His somewhat idealized but very popular depictions of village festivities known as the Kermess, present all sorts of amusing episodes in varied ways, nevertheless always showing a skilful integration of his dancers, musicians, womanisers, drunkards and debauchers in well-arranged scenes. Illustrative of the artist's

multi-faceted gifts are such different pictures as the *Group Portrait of the Magistrates and Arquebusiers of Antwerp*, the splendid *View in the Vicinity of Brussels*, the entertaining *Kitchen Seized by Monkeys* and *The Guardhouse*, in which Teniers displays equal skill as an exponent of the genre scene, landscape, animal painting and still life.

In the *Group Portrait of the Magistrates and Arquebusiers of Antwerp*, Teniers depicted the ceremony of honouring the dean of one of the two guilds attending the celebration — the arbalesters of St George's Company and the arquebusiers of St Sebastian's Company. Small in format, this picture is both a group portrait and a genre scene recording an event from the public life of Antwerp, and also an architectural landscape reproducing the appearance of buildings, a square and a street vista.

In *View in the Vicinity of Brussels*, one of his finest landcapes, the artist skilfully conveyed the sense of depth and air medium, subordinating details to the overall concept of the composition. Quite often Teniers painted amusing scenes in which animals, acting as protagonists, are engaged in human occupations (the idea harks back to classical fables and medieval literature). Thus, his *Kitchen Seized by Monkeys* shows the monkeys roasting meat on a spit, drinking wine, playing cards, and gossiping. The work does not carry any didactic message, being created merely for entertainment.

DUTCH ART: 17th CENTURY

W Early in the seventeenth century, as the outcome of a bourgeois revolution, seven northern provinces of the Low Countries shook off Spanish dominion and broke with the feudal system, to set up what was at that time most progressive state in Europe, the United Provinces, more commonly known as the Dutch Republic, or Holland. The rise of this new nation brought out, along with its economic and cultural advancement, the flourishing of art, and more specifically, painting. Though this small country had a population of no more than 2,500,000, hundreds of artists were active, many of whom achieved world stature. As a rule their pictures are small in scale, whence the term "the Little Dutch Masters" used by some art historians and critics. Destined to be hung on the walls of ordinary rooms in town or village, they reflect various aspects of contemporary Dutch life.

Hals. *Portrait of a Young Man with a Glove* (97, W-249) and *Portrait of a Man*

These two Hermitage paintings give a good idea of the innovative principles devised to reflect the surrounding world in a dynamic way as established by Frans Hals (1582—1666), one of the greatest seventeenth-century painters. He loved to convey the fleeting impression, and his brushwork was robust and unconstrained. Hals also worked on genre scenes, and in this field he trained several outstanding artists, among them Brouwer and Adriaen van Ostade.

Genre Painting

The popularity of genre painting in seventeenth-century Holland was an expression of the democratic trend in Dutch national art.
Characteristic of Jan Steen (1626—1679) was his entertaining, at times anecdotal, approach, as in *The Revellers*, *Physician Visiting a Sick Girl* and *Backgammon* (100, W-249), in which scrupulous attention to detail is skilfully blended with a well-integrated composition, and both colour and light-and-shade effects are excellently handled.
Two other genre painters, namely Pieter de Hooch (1629—1684) and Pieter Janssens (died in 1681), both of Delft, poeticized the burgher's life, subtly conveying the atmosphere of quiet comfort and the sedate and serene tenor of life in their town. Thus, whether in a scene outside a house (as, for example, in Hooch's *Mistress and Maidservant* (99, W-249) or in an interior, as in Janssens' *Room in a Dutch Home* (98, W-249), both convey light and space with great ease, thus imparting a particularly poetic charm to their pictures.
Refined elegance is characteristic of Gerard Terborch (1617—1681), who excels in conveying the resplendence and texture of fabrics. His

97

choice of colour combinations, as, for instance, in *A Glass of Lemonade* (101, W-249) and *Getting a Letter*, reveals faultless taste, while the use of an intense light to bring out the foreground is instrumental in adding to the expressiveness of his paintings.

In his early work — of which the Hermitage has a truly splendid example acquired by Peter the Great, *The Scuffle* (102, W-249) — Adriaen van Ostade (1610—1685) ridiculed the peasantry and their boorishness. However, in his later pieces, under the influence of Rembrandt, he displayed a certain sympathy for them, preferring to single out for attention their spiritual interests, as is exemplified by his canvas *Village Concert*.

W

98, 99
100, 101
102

Still Life Painting

Dutch painters preferred the term "still life" to the French *nature morte*, and, indeed, there is nothing dead about their pictures of such inanimate objects as wine-glasses, plates and dishes of various foodstuffs, as, for instance, in the pictures of Willem Claesz Heda (1594—1680/82) (104, W-249) and Pieter Claesz (1596/7—1661) (105, W-249), in which the disarranged dishes, crumpled table-cloth, partly filled wine-glasses and rind of a half-peeled lemon still bear the marks of having been touched by human hands.

Whether Heda, Claesz, or any other artist who practised still life painting, they all excelled in most accurately conveying the shape and solidity of objects, the stuff of which they were made and the reflections of light and colour on their surfaces. The diverse still lifes mounted for display include Balthasar van der Ast's bunches of fruit, Abraham van Beyeren's fish (103, W-249), and Matheus Bloem's dead game.

W

106
107

Landscape Painting

The Hermitage collection of Dutch landscape painting is widely representative. Thus, Jan Porcellis (*ca.* 1584—1632), an eminent marine painter, depicted the sea as seen off Dutch shores, skilfully generating the impression of turbulent waves, a fresh wind and the expanse of the sea, as, for instance, in his picture *Sea on a Cloudy Day*.

Meanwhile Jan van Goyen (1596—1656) made use of a near-monochrome palette in his epically serene yet peopled landscapes, such as *The Coast at Scheveningen* or *Winter Landscape*. Together with Julius Porcellis (*ca.* 1609—1645), Salomon van Ruysdael (1600—1670) and other seventeenth-century Dutch landscapists, he was responsible for the notable innovation of aerial perspective. Aert van der Neer specialized in complex lighting effects, while Paulus Potter (1625—1654) excelled in the painting of animals, as is distinctly manifest in his superb *Farm* (107, W-249).

The best of the eleven pictures in the possession of the Hermitage from the brush of the illustrious landscape painter Jacob van Ruisdael (1628/9—1682) is *The Marsh* (106, W-249), which amply demonstrates the ar-

108

tist's profoundly philosophical understanding of nature and carefully
conceived and highly expressive composition.

Rembrandt. *Flora* (108, W-254)

The greatest of all Dutch masters was, of course, Rembrandt Harmensz
van Rijn (1606—1669), of whose output the Hermitage boasts twenty-
five paintings as well as impressions of all his etchings.

After his marriage to Saskia van Uylenburgh in 1634, Rembrandt produced a series of portraits of her, one of which is *Flora*. Like the similarly conceived *Saskia in Arcadian Costume* (National Gallery, London),

W

it conforms to the genre of the pastoral portrait popular at the time. But whereas in the first Saskia is portrayed as an Arcadian shepherdess with wreathed head and holding a sceptre garlanded with grasses and flowers, in the Hermitage picture she is depicted as Flora, the Roman goddess of fertility, springtime and flowers. Rembrandt has not sought as yet to achieve an insight into human character, but merely reveals his admiration for the girlish Saskia in her fancy-dress; in this picture, like in his other highly decorative pieces of the period, coldish greens dominate in the overall colour scheme.

Rembrandt. *Danaë* (109, W-254)

This is without doubt one of the great master's best works. Though Rembrandt was familiar with pictures on the same theme that such Renaissance masters as Titian and Correggio had painted, and that depicted Danaë as the ideal of female beauty or stressed the erotic aspect of the ancient myth, he preferred to convey a mood of expectation, in which the noble feeling, the passion of love, is predominant. The unidealized body merely emphasizes the very human meaning Rembrandt brought to the theme.

110

Done in 1636, *Danaë* remained in the artist's house until *c.* 1646—47, when Rembrandt completely repainted its central part and thus brought the composition to its present-day form.

Rembrandt. *The Holy Family* **(110, W-254)**

The Hermitage version takes precedence over all other Rembrandts on the same theme. There was good reason for the other title, *The Carpenter's Family*, given to this painting, as the artist has set the biblical personages in the ordinary home of a Dutch craftsman, yet without reducing the scene to a mere genre episode. Pulsing with life, yet extraordinarily intimate, and painted in the predominantly golden tints beloved of the artist in the 1640s, with a splash of crimson to accentuate the figure of the Infant, *The Holy Family* is enchanting for the heartfelt mood of the story it tells and, at the same time, for its high degree of generalization, extolling accord within the home, maternal tenderness and affection. The high painterly merits allow this picture to be ranked among Rembrandt's finest.

111

Rembrandt. *David's Farewell to Jonathan* **(111, W-252)**

In the biblical story of David and Jonathan, King Saul, realizing that
David was more popular with the Israelites than his own son and heir
Jonathan, resolved to banish the former, to whom Jonathan was devoted. The choice of the theme of the sorrowful parting of two friends
was not fortuitous, as the artist's wife had just died, and the subject
was probably suggested by his own very personal tragedy. Thus Jonathan bears a resemblance to the artist (this is in fact the only oil self-
portrait of Rembrandt in the Hermitage), and the figure of David, depicted from the rear in such a way that his golden locks hide his
features, is highly reminiscent of Saskia. The overall spirit of deep
emotion, along with the exotic colour of the Orient and especially the

112

gold-embroidered robes, brightly illuminated against the dark and troubled sky, serve to associate this picture with other works that Rembrandt produced in the 1640s and that has conventionally been termed "Romantic".

Rembrandt. *Portrait of an Old Woman* (112, W-252)

More than half of the Hermitage Rembrandts are portraits. Painted in different years, they allow us to trace the evolution of this genre in the artist's work. About 1655 he painted a series of so-called portrait biographies. Rembrandt was particularly fascinated by the faces of elderly people as each of them was imprinted with the sitter's whole life. These include his *Portrait of an Old Man in Red* and *Portrait of an Old Woman.*

Rembrandt. *The Return of the Prodigal Son* (113, W-252)

This picture, one of Rembrandt's celebrated masterpieces, was painted shortly before his death. The parable of the son, who, unmindful of his father's advice, loses his health and money in debauch and orgy, and then, ruined, sick, weary and wretched returns home to be forgiven by his aged parent, attracted more than one artist. However, Rembrandt

W

has exceeded them all in his profound and wise interpretation which is concerned not with the prodigal son's riotous living or any homily on the evils of debauch, but with the tragedy of wasted life and man's readiness to help his fellow in the hour of need. The absence of movement and of external trappings compels the viewer to focus on the fates and emotions of the characters. With its deeply humanitarian message, this work may be regarded with good reason as the culmination of the great master's career.

114

GERMAN ART: 15th—19th CENTURIES

Of particular value in the relatively small collection are the paintings of the Renaissance masters Ambrosius Holbein and Lucas Cranach the Elder, which are exhibited in Room 264.

Holbein. *Portrait of a Young Man* (114, W-264)

The last of the extant works of Ambrosius Holbein (1495—1520), a talented artist who died at an early age, takes pride of place in the Hermitage collection of German painting of the period. The sitter is portrayed against the background of a cityscape, many elements of which such as the gates and the helmet-like tower are reminiscent of Milan's fortifications as depicted in a drawing by Leonardo da Vinci. The scrupulously determined lighting scheme is also an indication of Leonardo's influence. Renaissance features are especially manifest in the exact correspondence of human and architectural proportions. It is quite likely that the artist visited Lombardy. The colour range of the picture, with its predominance of deep browns, shows an affinity with the painter's more famous brother Hans Holbein. Efforts to decipher the monogram on the sitter's cap have so far proved unsuccessful. Judging by the Swabian costume with the slashed shoulders and the sword, the sitter was of noble blood, apparently a Swiss serving in Milan.

W

Cranach. *Venus and Cupid* (115, W-264)

This picture was painted in 1509, several years after Lucas Cranach the
Elder (1472—1553) moved to Wittenberg, a city where the impact of
the Italian Renaissance was keenly felt. There the artist met with hu-
manists and executed numerous, primarily secular, commissions. His
Venus and Cupid is the earliest extant work of German art depicting
the classical goddess nude, although historical records tell us that pictures of nude mythological personages adorned aristocratic homes as
early as the fifteenth century. Germans, unlike Italians, tended to re-
gard Venus as something of a *femme fatale*. In Nuremberg, which Cra-

116

nach is known to have visited, there were staged the so-called *Venus Spiel* pageants, when everyone transfixed with love's arrows had to obediently join her train. Such is the Venus that Cranach presents. Also somewhat equivocal is a moralistic Latin verse above the head of Venus, which reads: "Study with all your might to resist the voluptuous Cupid, / Lest blind love master your captive heart." Despite the showy warning, the sensual and the earthly are clearly felt in the picture. Italian influences are manifest in the artist's manner of execution and in his desire to make the figures stand out against a dark background.

Cranach. *The Virgin and Child* **(116, W-264)** **and** *Portrait of a Woman* **(117, W-264)**

With Cranach the Virgin above all symbolizes redemption, in contrast to the conception of the Italian artists, for whom she was, as a rule, the

W

117

personification of motherly love. Cranach was a friend of Luther — in fact he was even dubbed the first of Lutheran painters — and thus his Virgin concentrates within herself all the world's beauty and is portrayed against the backcloth of a joyous landscape. In effect, the picture connotes the main idea of the Lutheran faith. It is for the Virgin to atone for the sin that Eve committed — in much the same way as Christ's Calvary was the atonement for Adam's Fall. This message is intimated by two objects, the apple, symbolizing the Original Sin, and the crust of bread, symbolizing the body of the Lord, which the Infant Christ holds in his hands.

The complexity of the picture's content is characteristic of the Mannerist trends whose impact is especially evident in Cranach's later works, such as the *Portrait of a Woman*, also in the possession of the Hermitage.

118

Caspar David Friedrich (1774—1840), one of the most interesting German artists of the nineteenth century, is represented in the Hermitage by his typical works, Romantic landscapes extolling the beauty of his native land. They depict majestic mountain views (*Memories of the Riesengebirge, Morning in the Mountains*) and a splendid seashore in moonlight (*Moonrise over the Sea*) or in a misty haze.

Friedrich. *On a Sailing Ship* (118, W-342)

This painting is permeated with a sense of communion between man and nature. The landscape appears as perceived through the eyes of the young man and woman sitting in the prow of a sailing ship, who are spell-bound by the outlines of the spires and towers of a town looming through the misty air.

W

119

FRENCH ART: 15th—20th CENTURIES

The Hermitage collection of French art, exhibited in Rooms 272—297 on the first floor, and Rooms 314—332 and 343—350 on the second floor, is second only to that of the Louvre in richness and variety.

Limoges Enamels and Ceramics

The specific aspects of the technique of painted enamels, devised in the second half of the fifteenth century and differing from the earlier *cloisonné* enamels of the Middle Ages, wherein the metal bands were themselves an element of the design, caused the enameller to work more in the manner of a miniature painter, using the copper plate merely as a field upon which to depict detail and depth. The Limoges enamels, which are exhibited in Rooms 272 and 273, reveal a new Renaissance attitude to life, as is evidenced by the fifteenth-century ecclesiastical pieces and such highly decorative secular articles as dishes, plates and mirrors that were made in the next, sixteenth century — e.g. *Susannah and the Elders, The Boar Hunt*, a mug with round dance, and a jug with an allegorical depiction of Winter and Autumn.

120

Displayed in the same rooms is extremely rare Saint-Porchaire pottery (119, W-259). This French factory was active for no more than forty years, roughly between 1525 and 1565, manufacturing articles of absolutely no utilitarian purpose for a choice clientele. Here, the technique of inlaying patterns of strapwork in clays of contrasting colours, commonly known in French pottery, was brought to the heights of perfection. Earlier pieces are of a simple, concise form; later works imitate architectural motifs and show a rare elegance of minutely elaborate ornamentation.

Also of note is a dish by the Renaissance potter Bernard Palissy (1510—1589), whose characteristic interest in nature, coupled with his desire to reproduce it with the utmost fidelity, was evident even in the technique he employed. He made plaster casts of dead fishes, frogs, lizards and snakes to model what came to be known in France as *figulines rustiques*.

Le Nain. *The Milkmaid's Family* (120, W-276)

Realist tendencies in seventeenth-century French painting were revealed in the work of the Le Nain brothers, Antoine, Matthieu and especially Louis, who was the most talented of the three. Although the

121

figures in this picture, painted by Louis Le Nain in the 1640s, are static and separate, nonetheless compositionally they form a monolithic and majestic group. The artist's talent derives from a subtle understanding and knowledge of life, so each of his characters is strictly individualized. The peasants he has portrayed in this work are calmly confident of their own worth and possess a certain dignity. The landscape has been given a masterly treatment with light, precise brushstrokes — a single movement of the brush has been enough to represent the roadway. The elaborate, refined colour scheme is dominated by a silvery-greyish tone.

The modest pictures of the Le Nain brothers, remarkable for their true-to-life depiction of peasant families in their own humble environment, represented a significant achievement for the realist movement in French art.

Nicolas Poussin (1594—1665), the great seventeenth-century painter, who set on its way the Classicist trend in French art, followed a different road, refuting the genre picture, the portrayal of the everyday and the private. He sought by means of generalized and concise form to faithfully convey his elevated message, and to this end he took the heritage of classical antiquity and Raphael for his points of departure.

Poussin. *Tancred and Erminia* (121, W-279)

That the artist addressed himself to the episode in Torquato Tasso's *Ierusalem Delivered*, telling the story of how the knight Tancred is

122

rescued by his beloved Erminia, was by no means fortuitous. Indeed, he attached great significance to the choice of tale he set out to relate, a narrative which both lyrically and emotionally extols self-sacrifice. Poussin depicts the incident where Erminia takes up a sword to cut off her tresses to bandage Tancred's wounds. To correspond with the significance of the various personages the artist has selected red, blue and yellow respectively as the main colours for Tancred, Erminia and Vafrino the servant. The movement and disposition of each figure also impart characteristic, individualized detail, with Tancred stylishly elegant, the servant full of solicitous concern, and the ethereal Erminia impulsively decisive. The superbly painted sunset seems portentous and serves to heighten further the overall emotional impact of this picture.

By asserting humanitarian ideals Poussin made a major contribution to the advancement of French art.

Paintings by Claude Lorraine

Exclusively dedicated to landscape painting was another Classicist artist, the highly gifted Claude Lorraine (1600—1682), who was famed for his ability to convey subtle effects of light, space and perspective — as is reflected in *Morning, Noon, Evening* and *Night* of his *Four Times of the Day* cycle. The painting *Morning in a Harbour* (122, W-280) is also interesting.

123

French Applied Art

The Hermitage houses an exceptionally widely representative collection of silver, porcelain, tapestries, furniture and other objects of the decorative and applied arts of France.

The silver ceremonial services, snuff-boxes, ink-stands, candelabra and other objects reveal various techniques of metalwork; some pieces are set with porcelain, coloured stones or mother-of-pearl. One's attention is attracted by a silver centre-piece executed by the well-known Parisian craftsman Claude Ballin in 1724 (123, W-282).

Of special interest are tapestries from the *Caledonian Hunt* series (124, W-282) that were woven in Brussels from cartoons by the celebrated French artist Charles Lebrun (1619—1690), who headed the royal Gobelins factory and exercised a strong influence on the development of tapestry-making in Western Europe.

A splendid example of furniture is an ebony cabinet made at the Manufacture des Gobelins in the second half of the seventeenth century. Its elaborate design is a fine blend of architectural details, such as pilasters, niches and cornices, and sculptural ones as exemplified by the carved reliefs relating the Story of Joseph, or the legs shaped as caryatids. Such cabinets were also popular, even before France, in Italy, Germany and Flanders.

The greatest of the French ebonists active in the second half of the seventeenth and early eighteenth centuries, was André Charles Boulle (1642—1732), famous mainly for his innovations in marquetry. Be-

124

sides differently tinted woods, he made extensive use of bronze, copper, silver and tortoise shell plaques and also of lacquers. The Hermitage currently has in its possession only a few pieces by the master himself; one is a large ebony armoire (125, W-283).

Another unique piece of furniture is an elegant eighteenth-century Chinoiserie tortoise-shell side table of anonymous workmanship commissioned by the King of France as a present for the Queen of Portugal. Inlaid with gold and mother-of-pearl, it is also a fine example of the *piqué* technique — the tortoise-shell is studded with gold fillets in such a manner as to create a finely etched, dotted pattern. The subjects are executed in the Chinese style.

Sèvres porcelain ranks among the most famous and best ever produced in all of Western Europe. This celebrated French factory was founded in 1738 in the Château de Vincennes and in 1756 was moved to new premises at Sèvres, where the *pâte-tendre* (soft-paste) products were manufactured. Particular qualities of the paste and the fact that it was fired at a much lower temperature than hard paste served to promote its hand-painted decoration. The thickly laid pigments fused easily with the glaze to produce a particular gleam, brilliance and depth of colour. Indeed pieces with splendidly coloured grounds comprise some of the finest examples of Sèvres porcelain.

Other magnificent examples of Sèvres porcelain are: the *pot-pourri* vase (*vaisseau à mat*) made in the same year when the factory was moved to Sèvres; and the celebrated Cameo Service produced in 1778—79 on commission for Catherine the Great of Russia (some pieces

W

125

from it can be seen in the porcelain exhibition mounted in Rooms
269—271, where for the most part German wares from Meissen, Vienna,
Berlin and other centres are on display).
Particularly great popularity was enjoyed by the statuettes and groups
made of biscuit, an unglazed white porcelain. Involved in their output
were such eminent artists as Étienne-Maurice Falconet and François
Boucher, whose drawing was used to model the biscuit groups *Three
Graces Bearing Cupid* and *Jealousy*. French porcelain is also represented in the Hermitage collection by works from Arras, Tournai, Sceaux
and other provincial centres.

126

Watteau. *The Embarrassing Proposal* (126, W-284)
and *The Capricious Girl* (127, W-284)

The great French painter Antoine Watteau (1684—1721) rejected the
traditional historical and mythological themes in favour of subjects
drawn straight from the thick of life, preferring to paint actors and
soldiers, landscapes and genre scenes. His early genre painting of 1716,
Savoyard with His Marmot, already furnishes a lively, poetic characterization of a vagabond boy musician, whom circumstances have forced
to quit his native Savoy. This scene, glimpsed in real life, radiates a
sincere and sympathetic compassion for the ordinary man.

Especially popular were Watteau's works in the novel style he created,
known as the *fête galante*, which is well illustrated by his 1716 work,
The Embarrassing Proposal. No story is told and no direct message is
conveyed in this dreamland world wherein elegantly clad ladies and
their gallant admirers (often in imaginary costumes) are seen in a
conventionally treated, ideal scenic setting. His sensitive, vibrant brushwork produces a delicate glimmer: his figures, arranged in an integrated rhythmical pattern are casually graceful; their postures possess a
stylish elegance; their glances and movements are subtly fleeting.

In his *Capricious Woman*, which he painted about 1718, Watteau presents more than an idle flirtation — the amorous scene with all its ritual and conventions suggests a spirit of disillusionment and genuine

W

127

sadness. The unsteady highlights, the subtle play of tints and the delicate foliage through which a straw-yellow sky may be glimpsed impart a particular lyrical agitation to the scene.

Boucher. *Pastoral Scene* (128, W-285)

The greatest exponent of Rococo, which emerged in mid-eighteenth-century France, was François Boucher (1703—1770).

In this typical pastoral piece, Boucher, instead of providing us with a view of the French peasant's real life, leads us into a fairy-tale world

128

of studied elegance — though, true, his keen faculty for observation lends a genuine expressiveness to the scene in which a coldly calculating libertine seduces a naive and simple-hearted girl. It should likewise be noted that Boucher's work gives a clear indication of his fine decorative gifts.

His rustic landscapes well suited the glitter of palatial Rococo interiors. First Painter to the King, a member and, later, Director of the Royal Academy, Boucher was the supreme exponent of the Rococo style. Along with pictures, he produced decorative panels for palaces and mansions, and did cartoons for gobelins and other tapestries. He also made designs for the Royal Porcelain Works and theatres, was active as an engraver and illustrated books.

The eleven Bouchers kept in the Hermitage display a variety of genres. In addition to the *Pastoral Scene*, here reproduced, the collection includes *Landscape in Beauvais* and *Landscape with a Pond*, done in the 1740s, mythological scenes such as *The Triumph of Venus* and *The Toilet of Venus*, and allegorical companion paintings (probably part of a series of four canvases), *Cupids. Allegory of Painting* and *Cupids. Allegory of Poetry.*

Sculptures by Falconet

Conspicuous amidst the Rococo sculpture on display is the work of Étienne-Maurice Falconet (1716—1791), author of the famous monu-

W

129
130

ment to Peter the Great, the Emperor of Russia, to be seen today in Leningrad. While in France, having, as a rule, no serious commissions,
he confined his efforts to the creation of graceful, exquisite figurines
and statuettes, best known among which at the Hermitage are his
Flora (129, W-285) and *Cupid* (130, W-285).

131

Leading exponents of the new realist trend in French art associated with the ideology and outlook of the *tiers état* were the painter Jean-Baptiste-Siméon Chardin and the sculptor Jean-Antoine Houdon.

Chardin. *Grace Before Meat* (132, W-287) and *The Washerwoman* (131, W-287)

Central in the work of Jean-Baptiste Siméon Chardin (1699—1779) were genre scenes and still lifes, both of which were neglected in the time of flowering of pompous, formal art catering for the tastes of France's absolutist monarchy. In such paintings as *The Washerwoman* and *Grace Before Meat* (Room 287) he places in opposition to the ideals of the nobility those spiritual values that he discerned in the life of ordinary townsfolk, whose labours, customs, family relations and day-to-day surroundings he depicts with great skill. His small-scale pictures,

132

which are particularly intimate, gentle and poetic, and which possess a warmth and wealth of colour, mark a significant development of the realist tradition.

Houdon. *Voltaire* (133, W-387)

Jean-Antoine Houdon (1741—1828), the greatest of sculptors to come out of eighteenth-century France, repeatedly turned to the portrayal of his eminent contemporary, the writer and philosopher Voltaire. The culmination of his efforts is his own replica of the *Seated Voltaire* that he produced for the Comédie Française in Paris (displayed in Room 287). Refusing to portray the philosopher as the infirm and feeble old man he was when he sat for the sculptor, Houdon preferred to accentuate the aged Voltaire's greatness of thought. Draping the frail body within the sweeping folds of a loose cloak and imparting a stability of posture, Houdon focused attention on the philosopher's face and especially his eyes, getting them to convey the impression of shiny moistness by retaining in the chiselled and shaded pupils a tiny, protruding edge of marble to create the illusion of a highlight, which lends the glance a sense of profound perspecacity. An acid smile plays around the corners of the mouth, which, together with the eyes, makes the face seem alive.

The bourgeois Revolution of 1789—94 marked a turning-point in both the history and art of France. The chief exponent of the new trend of revolutionary Neo-Classicism that emerged in these years was Jacques Louis David (1748—1825). With the political, philosophical and aesthetic guide-lines of the Enlightenment as its point of departure, this art, which was anti-feudal in character, drew upon the heroes and themes of classical antiquity to defend the freedom of the individual as a citizen and member of society.

134

David. *Sappho and Phaon* (134, W-332)

This sole Hermitage David was painted in 1809 during the period of the First Empire when the artist was already breaking with the revolutionary Neo-Classical tradition. Though devoid of profound content, its integral composition, impeccable draughtsmanship and colouristic merits are indicative of David's outstanding mastery.

Gros. *Napoleon on the Bridge at Arcole* (135, W-331)

David's pupil, Antoine Jean Gros (1771—1835), chose for his subject a dramatic event that actually happened during the Battle of Arcole, when Napoleon, at a critical moment in the fighting, rushed forwards to lead his troops into the fray and wrested the bridge from the defending Austrian force. Though only Napoleon himself is depicted, we seem to sense the heat of the battle and the soldiers that surround him. Hence this is a history painting rather than a portrait. Furthermore, much in this painting — the sharply turned, diagonally disposed figure, the unfurled flag swirling in the wind, the highly contrasted play of light and shade, and finally the inner power that the heroicized Bona-

135

parte radiates — already conflicts with the rational and static manner
of Neo-Classicism, foretelling the advance of the new artistic trend of
Romanticism.

Paintings by Delacroix

The Hermitage possesses only two small pictures by Eugène Delacroix
(1798—1863), the major painter of the Romantic movement in France,
both of which are products of his later period, namely *Lion Hunt in
Morocco* (136, W-329) and *Arab Saddling His Horse*. Painted some
twenty years after he had travelled to Morocco and Algeria, they are

W

136

no faithful reproduction of the scenes observed and sketched while there — his notes were published, incidentally, later in his *Diary* — but rather an attempt to convey the exotic atmosphere, the flavour of the East with its untouched nature and bold and vigorous people. Unfettered by the canons of Classicism, Delacroix has created, in the first of the two pictures mentioned, a dynamic composition of heightened effects, in which the rules of perspective have been broken to bring the background closer and the figures of the hunters deformed to produce a sense of tension and the imminence of rapid movement. His brushwork is free and untrammelled. The colour scheme is all-important. The artist has employed local colours, half-tints and reflections, enhancing the expressiveness through the contrast of basic and complementary hues. Moreover, he has been able to catch the effect of light upon colour — adding blues and greens wherever the hunter's white shirt recedes into shadow. All these means have been used to unfold the romantic fervour of the episode portrayed.

Ingres. *Portrait of Count Guryev* (137, W-331)

Jean Auguste Dominique Ingres (1780—1867), an eminent exponent of Classicism, has portrayed the Russian diplomat Count Guryev against the background of a picturesque landscape in the neighbourhood of Florence. The facial features are most faithfully reproduced; indeed, the artist often painted rather ugly faces and never idealized the sit-

W

137

ter. But what is perhaps characteristic, is that even in the case of such a great, underivative master as Ingres, one senses in the Classicist portrait, with its well-balanced centric composition, triangular structure, emphasis on line, and smooth texture, the indisputable impact of the Romantic movement as expressed in an attempt to convey the individual features of the sitter, to stress the instability of Nature in the approaching storm and to build up an intense colour scheme.

Throughout the 1830s and 1840s, the realist trend began to make headway in its rebellion against the official Classicist style and likewise

W

138

against the Romantic movement with its tendency towards fantasy and exoticism. There appeared what was known as the Barbizon school, a group of landscape painters, led by Théodore Rousseau (1812—1867), who left their Paris studios for the village of Barbizon in the Forest of Fontainebleau, where they sought to depict the unprettified scenery of France.

Rousseau. *The Countryside near Granville* (138, W-328)

This picture, painted in 1833, shows the outskirts of a seaside town. By leaving the entire foreground empty and exhaustively detailing the background, Rousseau has attempted to draw the viewer into the depths of the composition, and impart a fuller sense of the unexceptional character of this deserted spot, lost among cliffs and woodland. Proceeding from plein-air sketches, with brilliant visual memory, the artist has sought in this studio-painted picture to convey all the inimitable charm of unadorned Nature.

Paintings by Dupré, Diaz, Daubigny and Troyon

Although the Barbizon school adhered to one common method, this did not rule out difference in their individual styles. Thus, Jules Dupré (1811—1889) gave his landscapes a more emotional treatment than Rousseau, and the colourful impasto of his *Rustic Landscape* (139,

W-328) and *Landscape with Cows* conveys admirably Nature's elemental force.

The desolate landscapes of Diaz de la Peña (1808—1876) with their solitary trees and lonely travellers. (140, W-328) generate a plaintively Romantic atmosphere of nostalgia. Such landscapes by Charles François Daubigny (1817—1878) as *The Banks of the Oise* (141, W-322) and *Pond and River Bank*, with their large expanses of sky reflected in still sheets of water, seem full of air and light.

W

141
142

143

In one version of his picture *On the Way to the Market* (142, W-324), painted in 1859, Constant Troyon (1810—1865) displays admirable talent as a painter not only of landscapes, but also of animals, conveying with virtuoso facility a herd on the move in the morning haze.

Millet. *P easant Women Carrying Firewood* (143, W-321)

Jean-François Millet (1814—1875) attained the height of his creative powers in the village of Barbizon, where he lived for twenty-five years until his death. As one of the leading realists in French art, he revived the painting of peasant subjects that the Le Nain brothers had introduced, and was the first to portray the peasant's daily struggle for survival with great sympathy and convincingness. He sought, as he himself put it, "to direct men's thoughts towards the sad lot of mankind, the burden of toil."

In *Peasant Women Carrying Firewood*, painted around 1858, the characterizations of the figures overshadow the genre aspect. A profound

144

feeling is revealed for the sluggish, heavy rhythm of the movements of the peasant women depicted, their backs bent and straining under their loads. The doleful colour range, terse composition and generalized treatment of form lend an austere monumentality to this small picture.

Landscapes by Corot

Jean-Baptiste Camille Corot (1796—1875), besides painting portraits and genre pieces, created what may be termed "the landscape of mood" of which the Hermitage boasts seven examples. Radiating a subtly lyrical spirit of harmony, these small pictures — among them, *Landscape with a Lake, Peasant Woman Pasturing a Cow on the Edge of a Wood* (144, W-321) and *Pond in a Forest* — eloquently attest to his characteristic style. The colour scheme of silvery greys. the virtuoso use of tonal values and the depiction of such atmospheric phenomena as haze, mist, fog and twilight, all serve to enhance the poetic charm of these impressions of various restful corners of the Île-de-France.

145

The 1870s witnessed the emergence in French art of a new movement, that of Impressionism. The Impressionists placed the emphasis on painting outdoors, on the basis of direct visual "impressions". Claude Monet may be considered the founder of this method.

Monet. *Lady in the Garden at Sainte-Adresse* (145, W-319)

Lady in the Garden, painted in 1860, is the earliest of the eight pictures by Claude Monet (1840—1925), that the Hermitage has in its collection. The artist handles in it the effects of daylight in an entirely new manner, recording not the actual, constant colour of the object depicted, but rather that of the first visual impression, as perceived at that particular moment in the sunlight. The freely, seemingly dashed-on strokes of pure colour convey the general sensation one would get when viewing the actual scenery as lit by light through an atmospheric medium from some distance away.

Again, in the cheerful *A Corner of the Garden at Montgeron* painted in 1876—77 (147, W-319) and *The Haystack at Giverny* (1886), two landscapes seen in the diffused lighting of a cloudy day, the separate patches of pure colour have been laid on separately in such a way as to fuse with one another when viewed from a distance.

The same features characterize other works by the Impressionists, such as the paintings *Boulevard Montmartre* by Camille Pissarro (146, W-318),

W

146
147

W

150

Child with a Whip by Auguste Renoir (148, W-320), and River Banks at Saint-Mammes by Alfred Sisley (149, W-319).

Renoir. *Portrait of the Actress Jeanne Samary* (150, W-320)

Unlike most of his Impressionist friends, Auguste Renoir (1834—1917) was rather interested in genre scenes, nudes and portraits than in

W

151

landscapes. Combining plein-air sketches with studio painting, he focused on the human being and the happier, brighter sides of life around him.

In this portrait of Jeanne Samary, an actress of the Comédie Française, painted in 1878, Renoir did not strive for a deep, many-sided characterization of the sitter, but preferred to record a fleeting impression with barely perceptible nuances of feeling and mood, as expressed in the actress's bright eyes, elusive smile, incomplete gesture and light movement. By means of soft but dynamic brushwork, he has conveyed the warmth of the body, along with the complex tints and reflection on the pinkish-yellow dress. In his *Girl with a Fan* painted in 1881, Renoir achieves, through the use of glazing, the shimmering, fresh and radiant effect of colouring.

Pastels by Degas

Another Impressionist who did few landscapes and preferred to work in his studio rather than out of doors, painting mostly portraits and genre scenes, was Edgar Degas (1834—1917). Less interested in the ef-

W

fects of light and air — all-important for the landscape painter — he gave equal attention to colour and draughtsmanship. He drew subject matter for his works from the life of contemporary Paris. His enthusiasm for the movement, the gesture and the plasticity of the body led him to produce a great many nudes, often painted in pastel.

The Degas nudes in the possession of the Hermitage, such as *After the Bath* (151, W-320), were executed in the 1880s. They show a clear break with academic canon, according to which the naked body should be depicted as the ideal of beauty. Veracity was the point of departure to which he faithfully adhered and in place of traditional static postures, he provides unusual views, from above or from the side, of natural, fleeting movement, stressing the spontaneity of this "casual", unpremeditated composition by moving the figure away from a central position, or even abruptly cutting off a part of the figure with the frame. The works of Degas are truly striking in their unexpectedness and acuteness of vision.

In the pastel *After the Bath* the woman's figure is depicted without any attempt to beautify or to distract with details. Her uncomfortable and precarious pose is so convincing that the scene appears not as deliberatley constructed but as taken directly from life.

Such masters of the late nineteenth century as Cézanne, Van Gogh and Gauguin fell under the spell of the Impressionist movement in the

153

early stages of their painting careers. Later, however, they each followed their own path, and although in their evolution of new artistic
forms they frequently abandoned conventional means of expression,
rejecting linear perspective, tending to deform objects and heighten the
expressiveness of line and colour, nonetheless they revealed in these
departures a profound understanding of the artistic means of expression that the exponents of previous trends and movements had employed. In their work they sought to achieve a synthesis of monumental
and decorative effect.

Thus Paul Cézanne (1839—1906), while sharing the Impressionist view
that it was necessary to study Nature, was against capturing merely
the chance, fleeting moment, which, due to constant change, obscured
such essential qualities as dimension, structure and solidity.

Cézanne. *The Banks of the Marne*
(152, W-318)

Cézanne depicts reality as solid and durable, with his colour scheme
based on contrasts, thus developing and transforming the Impressionist
technique of colour separation. Whereas in Claude Monet's pictures, for
instance his *Pond at Montgeron* (1888), water is an unstable, changeable element, whose surface ripples endlessly, by contrast Cézanne's
landscape of 1876 is static, with the Marne, mirror-like, reflecting the

154

buildings and trees lining its banks in such a way that the reflection seems just as real as the solid, material world. While with Monet the trees seem to dissolve in the shimmering, sun-shot atmosphere, with Cézanne they are perceived as a unified and tangible mass. By excluding every changeable, chance element, Cézanne creates an overall integrated image of Nature. Resorting to but a meagre palette of greens, blues, oranges and reds, which he places in opposition to one another, he has been able to produce the impression of the solidity of form and of the clarity of space.

Cézanne. *Still Life with Drapery* (153, W-318)

Unlike the Impressionists, Cézanne favoured the still life, towards which he adopted an approach, fundamentally different to those of preceding generations of artists. His aim was not truth to appearance; he was not interested in rendering reality as a visualized surface but preferred to simplify and geometrize the shapes of objects, thereby disclosing their basic structural elements and achieving convincing solidity. His *Still Life* of 1899, though devoid of the freshness and flavour of Nature's bounties, nonetheless presents each piece of fruit — which it is at times difficult to identify — as a part of one integral material world that possesses form, depth and weight. However, to achieve this, Cézanne has not used the effects of light and shade that his predecessors applied, but has modelled colour itself to produce the impression of tangibility and volume. His specific choice of colours in this work — the orange reds of the fruits and the blue-whites of the napkins — emphasizes the visible shape; hence there is no longer need to rely on line.

Cézanne. *The Smoker* (154, W-318)

In his portraits Cézanne often approached the sitter in the same way as he did a still life, with the aim of obtaining a plastic expressiveness

156

and sculpturesque clarity of image. Thus, in *The Smoker*, painted in 1895, despite the simplifying generalization, as expressed, for instance, in the use of dark splashes of colour in place of the eyes, he has been able to convey the peasant's mood of inner concentration and the rigidity of his figure, seeming to personify the stability and permanence of provincial life.

Paintings by Van Gogh

The Hermitage has in its collection only later works by Vincent van Gogh (1853—1890), who, unlike the Impressionists, did not strive to record the purely visual impression, but sought to evolve new means of conveying his own emotional state. The means of expression he employs are intensified to the extreme, the heightened colour combinations enhance the emotional impact of the overall colour scheme, the drawing is expressively tense, and even the texture of his violent brushwork has become an effective means of communicating to the viewer the picture's dramatic content and mood. Moreover, this was no superficial technique. Thus, in his *Lilac Bush* (155, W-317), one of the Van Goghs in the Hermitage collection, the artist presents the shrub in movement, its sprouting, growth and flowering, with the blue-green palette exuding an amazing freshness. Meanwhile in the landscape

Cottages with Thatched Roofs (156, W-317), the highly expressive linear pattern and forceful brushwork, revealing the painter's passionate emotionality, introduce a mood of foreboding into this representation of what might seem a quiet and restful haven.

Paintings by Gauguin

The fifteen pictures that the Hermitage possesses by Paul Gauguin (1848—1903) relate to the period of his life spent on Tahiti, in an attempt not only to flee civilization but also to steep himself in the life and culture of other peoples. Such pictures of the 1890s as *Tahitian Pastoral Scenes* (157, W-316), *Woman Holding a Fruit* and *The Idol* were the offspring of his desire to comprehend the outlook, beliefs, art and folklore of the Polynesians. However, these are rather a poeticized expression of admiration for the Tahitian exoticism than any reflection of the actual life of the Maori.

The specific features of Gauguin's style are his simplification of form and the subordination of every element to a strictly conceived decorative pattern. He discarded light-and-shade effects and subtle colouristic nuances in favour of a consonance of pure colours in an attempt to heighten contour and linear rhythm. In his paintings he used only details from nature studies, but his work clearly reflects tendencies that were typically Post-Impressionistic, notably the search for monumental integrity and symbolic generalization.

W

158

Sculptures by Rodin

Many of the eleven works by the celebrated French sculptor Auguste
Rodin (1840—1917) displayed in Room 315, such as *Eternal Spring* (158,
W-315), *Romeo and Juliet, Cupid and Psyche,* and *The Poet and the
Muse,* are consonant with Impressionist painting, and in his enthusiasm
for lighting effects, he often indulged in soft delicate modelling of
marble, creating flowing forms to produce the impression of a tenderly
gleaming nude body bathed in the surrounding air.

Of a considerable interest is a signed plaster version of the famous
sculpture *The Bronze Age* (159, W-315), which provoked a riot in the
Salon of 1877. The advocates of traditional art with their adherence to
canons and idealization of the image rebuked Rodin for his vivid and
spontaneous treatment of the human body.

Among the other works by Rodin that should be mentioned are the
marble bust of Varvara Yeliseyeva, the bronze head of a *Man with a
Broken Nose* and the plaster bust of the Japanese dancer Hanako.

W

160

W

Paintings by Matisse

One of the new trends in twentieth-century French art was Fauvism.
Its name stems from the French word *fauve* meaning wild beast — the
derisive epithet was given to a group of artists represented at the
Paris Salon d'Automne of 1905. Though the Fauves had no clear-cut
theoretical platform, they rejected tradition and declared that they
were governed solely by their own emotions; they emphasized colour
as dominant in painting and strove for a markedly decorative effect.
After the group disintegrated each member followed his own path.
The greatest of the Fauves was Henri Matisse (1869—1954), who sought,
as he himself phrased it, "the possibility of expression beyond the limits
of literal imitation". Dominant in his method is the use of quite conventional yet pure colour of extraordinary vividness, especially when
juxtaposed with a patch of some other colour. To enhance the vibrancy
of his colour scheme, Matisse rejected modelling, texture, lighting
contrasts and transitional tonal values, imparting great significance to
contour lines around the diverse areas of colour, lines which seem to
construct the figure or object on the flat surface of the canvas, create
the impression of movement and rhythm, and produce a vivid decorative effect — as is eloquently evidenced by his *Family Group* of 1911
(162, W-347), *The Red Room* (1908), *Conversation* (1909), *The Dance*
(160, W-346), painted in 1910, *Music* (1910), and *Portrait of the Artist's
Wife* of 1913 (161, W-347).
Matisse either transforms or completely abjures the traditional elements of compositional construction; his pictures are lacking depth

146

W

162

and air, his forms are schematic and simplified, so some of his works are quite reminiscent of decorative panels. Even in pictures in which nothing seems to be happening and people and objects are merely juxtaposed in one way or another, nonetheless the interplay of line and colour generates an inner relationship.

The unique character of Matisse's art derives from his unusual imagery and the strikingly terse and blunt construction of his pictures. The thirty-seven canvases by Matisse in the possession of the Hermitage Museum, all painted in the years before the outbreak of the First World War, present a fairly good idea of the artist's buoyant, life-asserting work.

Paintings by Picasso

Although Pablo Picasso (1881—1973) is well represented in the Hermitage collection, all of his thirty-seven works date to the early stages in his complex and chequered career, so indicative of the sharp contradictions of the twentieth century. Well versed in cultural tradition, especially of his native Spain, Picasso, after arriving, at the turn of the century, in Paris, then the forefront of world art, initiated his search for novel approaches to painting.

The earliest of the Hermitage works by Picasso, *Absinthe Drinker* (163, W-344), painted in 1901, together with several of his pictures executed between 1901 and 1904 — his Blue Period — and during the subsequent

163

Rose Period, demonstrate an interest in the sad lot, loneliness and suffering of the disinherited and the dispossessed. Even when he turned to themes no longer novel in French art, such as cafés and their clientele, reality was markedly transformed. As a rule, one is unable to identify the nationality, occupation or period of the people portrayed in either the *Absinthe Drinker* or other concurrently produced pieces. Nonetheless the laconic simplified imagery imparts great expressiveness to them, while the deliberate deformation of the figures and the conventional colour scheme serve to heighten the dramatic effect of the works and infuse them with profound emotion.

W

164

One of Picasso's Rose Period efforts is the poetically plaintive *Boy with a Dog* (164, W-345) which was painted in 1905. Although the palette of pinks and blues, and the graceful limpid drawing with its delicate modelling, amplify the scene's naturalness and sense of motion, there is nothing novel here, as at this stage of his artistic career Picasso had not yet transcended the framework of nineteenth-century tradition.

165

Fundamentally new approaches emerged when Picasso became an exponent of that new movement in twentieth-century French art that has
come to be known as Cubism, and whose advocates united in 1908 in
the Bateau-Lavoir group. The Hermitage Picassos enable the viewer to
trace the two — analytical and synthetic — stages of Cubist expression
in the artist's work. The first stage was marked by his striving to ana-
lyze the inner form and structure of the human figure or of objects;

151

W

166

thus in the picture that he painted in 1909, *A Woman with Mandoline* (165, W-345), the shapes of real objects are still recognizable, but in place of emotional vision the artist conveys his message by means of geometrized forms. In works done during the second phase, such as *Musical Instruments*, painted in 1912, Picasso broke form down into various structural elements and separate planes which he then reconstituted into intricate rhythmical patterns. In 1914 the artist abandoned Cubist experiment in favour of other directions.

Landscapes by Marquet

The art of France's leading twentieth-century landscape painter Albert Marquet (1875—1947) represents an organic whole despite his fusion of innovation with adherence to realist tradition. His short-lived intimacy with the Fauves consolidated his desire to express himself through the use of simplified form, bright splashes of colour and laconic contours. The fact that he concentrated on a few basic elements selected from his direct visual perception of Nature explains the extremely sparse use of means of expression in his pictures, which are, as a rule, limited to but one tonality. In Marquet's landscapes the beholder can always tell the season, time of day and weather. In his views of Paris, his impressions of well-known places — for instance, *Quai du*

167

Louvre and the Pont-Neuf in Paris (1906), *View of the Seine and Monument to Henri IV* painted about 1907 (166, W-350) and *A Rainy Day in Paris (Notre-Dame)* (167, W-350) — the artist presents the great city as a fresh and lyrical impression.

Paintings by Léger

Noticeable among works by twentieth-century French painters are paintings by Fernand Léger (1881—1955), an artist who was also engaged in monumental painting, mosaics, stained glass and ceramics. He had passed through an infatuation with Cubism and remained an adherent

153

W

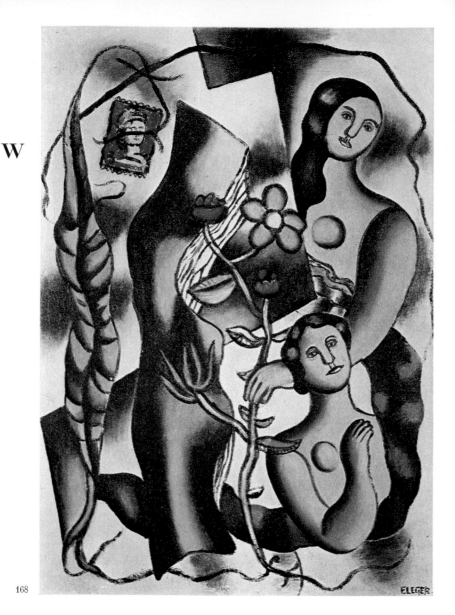

168

ELEGER.

of conventional imagery, yet he had never lost a life-asserting attitude to reality. His *Carte Postale* of 1932—48 (168, W-350) is a complex and at the same time lucidly harmonious work remarkable for its rhythmic compositional pattern. The seemingly fragmented details make up a single monumental and optimistic image.

ENGLISH ART: 17th — 19th CENTURIES

Conspicuous in the relatively small exhibition, mostly of portraits and landscapes, displayed in Rooms 298—302, are the works of two great English painters, Joshua Reynolds and Thomas Gainsborough.

Reynolds. *The Infant Hercules Strangling the Serpents* (169, W-299)

Joshua Reynolds (1723—1792) borrowed the theme for this picture, which was commissioned by Catherine the Great of Russia, from the myth related by the ancient Greek poet Pindar. Hera, the jealous spouse of Zeus, the supreme deity, persecutes the infant Hercules, the son of Zeus from Alcmena, wife of Amphitrion, the King of Thebes, by depositing two serpents in his cradle. The frightened mother is overjoyed when she sees the mighty infant strangle the snakes with his bare hands. As Reynolds himself observed, he had chosen the supernatural strength of the infant Hercules as the subject because it allowed for

W

170

comparison, albeit remote, with the renowned, but by no means child-like, strength of the Russian Empire. Many of the faces are of well-known contemporaries of the artist: thus the features of the old sooth-sayer Tiresius, who predicted a glorious future for Hercules, were re-cognizable as those of the artist's friend, the noted English man of let-ters, Dr. Samuel Johnson, while jealous Hera, who from behind the clouds overlooks her act of vengeance, bears a resemblance to the cel-ebrated English actress Sarah Siddons. Skilful use is made of a large scale of composition, varied foreshortening, light-and-shade contrasts and other Baroque devices. The picture so greatly pleased the Russian Empress that, in addition to the fee, she sent the painter a gold snuff-

W

171

box with her portrait skirted by large diamonds, and hung the painting
in the Hermitage.
At about the same time Reynolds painted for Prince Grigory Potiomkin
another two pictures, namely, *The Continence of Scipio*, and *Cupid Un-
tying the Girdle of Venus*.

Gainsborough. *Portrait of a Lady in Blue* (170, W-300)

The name of the lady portrayed by Thomas Gainsborough (1727—1788)
in this picture, the only one that the Hermitage has in its collection by
this artist, indeed its finest specimen of English art, is something we
do not know to this day. The inspired face, elegant gesture and serene
posture serve to emphasize her noble refinement. The exquisite combination of the pinks of the tender face with the silvery blues, whites
and greys of the powdered coiffure, dress and scarf is indicative of the
artist's masterly handling of colour. His individual technique of ap-
plying a limpid layer of diluted colour to secure an impression of
ethereal grace, coupled with his rapid and fine brushwork, and his
extraordinarily subtle use of transitional tonal values, all impart a poetic
charm to his work.

157

Pottery by Josiah Wedgwood

In 1774 the most distinguished English potter Josiah Wedgwood (1730—
1795) made for Catherine the Great of Russia the celebrated Green Frog
Service (172, 173; W-300), the name of which derives from the facetious
coat of arms of a green frog enclosed within a triangular shield that is
to be found on each piece — deriving, in turn, from the name of the
site of "La Grenouillère" Palace (later renamed the Palace of Chesme),
for which the service was commissioned — Frog Bog. The decoration,
executed in brown on a cream-white ground, consists of 1,244 English
landscapes incorporating stately homes or old buildings.
Also on display in the same room are some other pieces by Wedgwood:
medallions (171, W-300), ornamental plaques and vases.

# Culture and Art of the Peoples of the East

Interest in Eastern artefacts arose in Russia long ago; the first Russian museum, Peter the Great's *Kunstkammer* (Cabinet of Curios), housed a large number of Oriental coins, and a series of prominent works of art from Graeco-Bactria, Syria and Achaemenid Persia. Catherine II had a collection of glyptics that included engraved gems from Ancient Egypt, Mesopotamia, Parthia, Sassanian Iran, Byzantium and China. Apparently in the 1770s, Admiral Grigory Spiridov brought from the Archipelago a Byzantine marble slab depicting circus scenes, and some relics of classical antiquity. Also around this time Sassanian and Byzantine silver vessels were found at Sludka, a village in Perm Province. All these items later formed the basis of the Hermitage Oriental collections.

The Oriental Department, which boasts today the USSR's largest collection of its kind of more than 155,000 items illustrating the culture and art of the peoples of the East, and which was started in 1920, currently occupies ground-floor Rooms 34—66, 68—69, 80—96 and 100, and second-floor Rooms 351—371, 375—376 and 381—397.

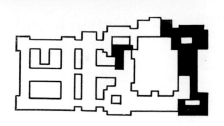

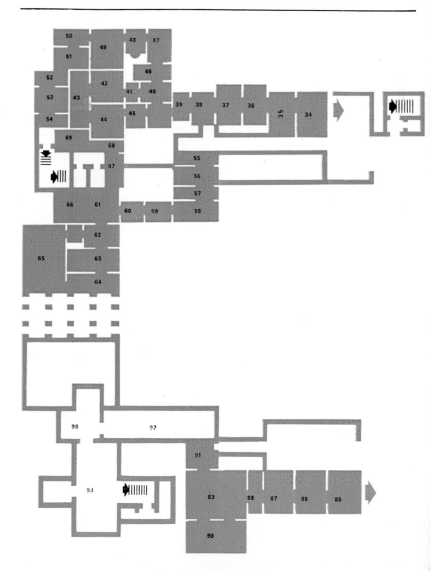

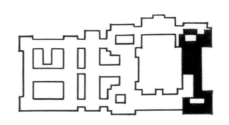

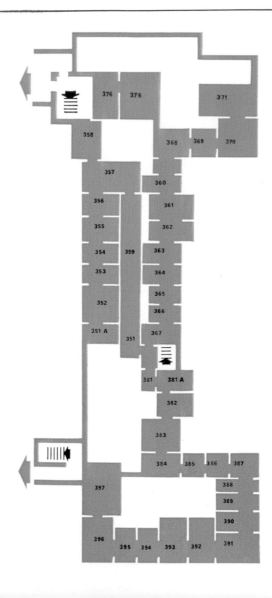

CULTURE AND ART OF ANCIENT EGYPT

The primitive flint implements from Neolithic Nile delta communities, which are some 6,000 years old, are the earliest of the artefacts in the Egyptian collection. Indeed, thanks to excavations carried out in Egypt in 1961—63 by a team of Soviet archaeologists led by Academician Boris Piotrovsky in the area destined for flooding under the Aswan Dam project, such finds as clay untensils, a flint knife, sickle blades, a mortar for pounding grain and several other objects, all discovered on a site presumed to have been an ancient cattle range, were added to the Hermitage store. These tools illustrate the development of farming, handicrafts, hunting, art and religion, as well as tribal strife in pre-Dynastic Egypt.

Funerary Reliefs

Art underwent a radical change, with the human being becoming its chief concern, during the period of the Old Kingdom — from approximately 3,000 to 2,400 B.C., when Egypt was unified into one state under the rule of Pharaoh.
The exhibited stone reliefs, which are from the tombs of the Egyptian nobility, had originally been painted. The character of the portrayals and the composition suggest a well-developed artistic canon. Thus, if we take the carved relief from the tomb of one Nimaatra, we shall see that the figure of the enthroned dignitary is several times larger than those of his servants, arranged in rows or friezes, one above the other, who wait on him. The unknown sculptor has displayed a considerable degree of proficiency in integrating the different parts of the figure which are slanted at different angles, the head and the feet in profile, and the eyes, shoulders and chest, in full face. These monumental, decorative reliefs wcre included in the overall scheme of funerary architecture to break the monotony of the walls. Though deriving from religious notions of an afterlife, they nonetheless record many interesting observations from reality.
Another relief, from the tomb of the courtier Meryre-ankh, reveals a different technique of execution with the figure cut into the stone. The inscriptions are good examples of ancient hieroglyphics.

Statue of Amenemhet III (174, E-82)

One magnificent piece of sculpture in the Hermitage collection is the granite statue of the Pharaoh Amenemhet III (1850—1800 B.C.), who reigned over Egypt during the period of the Middle Kingdom (21st — 18th centuries B.C.) Although idealized and conventional, it nevertheless betrays its creators' desire to convey such individual features as the deeply-set narrow eyes and the high cheekbones. The firmly compressed thin lips and jutting chin impart a stern and imperious cast to

the face. And the characteristic headdress with its representation of the *uraeus*, the sacred asp, the guardian and protector of the ruler, and likewise the three names of the Pharaoh, inscribed within the cartouche on the throne, are reminders that before us is the potentate of all Egypt. The sculptor has displayed a fine feeling for the medium, making skilful use of the play of light and shade on the granite's surface.

Ushabti Figurines

E Also on display here are what are known as the *ushabti*, small carved wooden figures of servants, coated with plaster and painted, that were placed in the tombs of their aristocratic overlords.

Papyrus Manuscripts

The Hermitage papyrus manuscripts, namely *The Tale of the Shipwrecked Man*, *The Prophecy of Neferti* and *The Instructions of the Pharaoh of Herakleopolis to His Son Merikare*, are priceless, world-famous examples of ancient Egyptian literature. The first is the story of an Egyptian sailor, who, at the outcome of a shipwreck, finds himself stranded on the island of a fantastic serpent. When the sailor, fulfilling the serpent's prophecy, leaves the island with a menagerie of outlandish beasts and birds, the island sinks into the watery depths. The second papyrus, *The Prophecy of Neferti*, presents a historical chronicle illustrating the social changes that Egypt was undergoing at the time of writing.

Mut-Sekhmet Statue (175, E-86)

Among the many relics dating back to the period of the New Kingdom (16th — 11th centuries B.C.), when Egypt was the greatest power of the East, there are at the Hermitage several noteworthy statues, in particular that of the lion-headed goddess Mut-Sekhmet, daughter of the supreme deity Ra, the Sun-God, and herself goddess of war and blazing heat. The sculptor has sought here to stress the human being's power which is compared to the strength of a wild beast.

Legend has it that the goddess, furious with the humans who refused to obey her senile father, resolves to kill them by the scorching heat of a drought. Only the intercession of other, compassionate deities who advise the humans to flood the area, under cover of darkness, with beer dyed red, which the angry goddess drinks the following morning, mistaking it for human blood, saves them from complete extermination. The myth is based on reality — the waters of the Nile, turning red as they burst their banks, saved the people of Egypt from drought. The forbidding goddess holds in her hands the life-giving symbol of life — the *ankh*. This monumental statue sculpted during the reign of Amenhotep II, whose name is inscribed on the throne, once stood amidst similar statues adorning the famous Karnak Temple.

E

175

E

176

Fayum Portraits (176, E-90)

The burial cult is illustrated also by the Fayum portraits, so called after the oasis of Fayum where the first such portrait was discovered.
This kind of portraiture blossomed during the first three centuries of
the Christian era, when Egypt was part of the Roman Empire. Exe-

E

177

cuted by means of wax pigments on wooden panels, or sometimes in tempera on fabric, these portraits were kept in Egyptian homes and after the demise of their owners were bandaged onto mummies as a kind of face mask.

Coptic Textiles

The Hermitage collection of Coptic textiles is world-famous for its richness and variety. Hand-woven of wool and linen between the fourth and ninth centuries, at a time when Graeco-Egyptian features were merging with early-Christian and Byzantine elements in the country's culture, these textiles are astounding for their highly diversified range of decoration and design, incorporating representations of mythological deities, animals, fantastic creatures, plants as well as various ornamental patterns, and, in later examples, stories and symbols borrowed from the Christian religion. Of interest is also a textile depicting the Goddess of Earth (177, E-90).

E

178

CULTURE AND ART OF CHINA

The Hermitage collection of objects illustrating Chinese culture and art is the largest in the Soviet Union — though, true, very early artefacts are relatively few and occupy only the first small room. These include bones used in the thirteenth and twelfth centuries B.C. for practising scapulimancy, a type of divination, and also bronzes, textiles, lacquers, rubbings on paper from stone reliefs of the Han dynasty period — the third century B.C. to the third century A.D. — and many other items illustrating the development of writing, beliefs, arts and handicrafts.

A significant contribution to the study of Chinese culture was made by the field expeditions of the Russian Orientalists Sergei Oldenburg, Dmitry Klementz and the Berezovsky brothers, Mikhail and Nikolai. The artefacts they discovered and brought from the expeditions — displayed in Room 359 — are representative of the culture of Sinkiang oasis kingdoms of the first to twelfth century.

179

Tun Huang Relics

Exhibited in Room 351a are finds made by Academician Sergei Oldenburg on his second Turkestan expedition of 1914—15. Among them are
fragments of wall paintings executed by means of vegetable and animal pigments on loess and size-coloured figurines of deities and monks
from the Monastery of the Cave of the Thousand Buddhas — founded
in 366 A.D. some twenty kilometres away from the provincial town of
Tun Huang in Sinkiang. Remarkable among the sculpted pieces are the
two huge fabulous beasts (178, E-351a) of unfired clay that stood guard
on either side of the enthroned Buddha.

Khara-Khoto Artefacts

A considerable part of the display consists of finds made in 1907—9 by
the Russian archaeologist Piotr Kozlov while excavating on the fringes
of the Gobi desert among the ruins of the Tangutan city of Khara-Kho-
to, laid waste by Ghenghis Khan in 1226. The tools, textiles, garments,
ceramics and books unearthed furnish a many-sided picture of life in
this city. Kozlov's finds also included examples of painting, such as *The
Deity of the Moon* (180, E-352), painted on paper in the twelfth century,
a period of the flowering of art in the Tangutan state Hsi-Hsia.

E

Porcelain

The porcelain that was made in China in the eighth and ninth centuries, one thousand years before similar ceramic wares were produced
in Europe, naturally takes pride of place in the display. Greatly prized
was the jade-like *celadon* ware, exquisite porcelain painted in bright
enamel colours — *The Lion of Fo* (181, E-355), and porcelain with fine
underglaze painting in cobalt blue — *Dish* (182, E-355). The vase with
a representation of a blossoming plum-tree (179, E-355) was used for
the delivery of New Year presents. The ceremony generally took place

in spring when the plum-tree was in bloom, and the depiction of its flowers symbolizes a wish of beauty, youth and happiness.

Exhibits from the heyday of porcelain production are the seventeenth- and early eighteenth-century *famille-verte* wares, with a painted, five-colour, but predominantly green, decoration, and *famille-rose* wares, whose colour scheme centres on a gentle pink.

Lacquerwork

E Luxury items of carved lacquer — made from the sap of the *rhus ver-nicifera* tree — were usually of a vermilion red, but occasionally as many as five or six other colours were applied, especially black. The articles produced — side tables, screens, or boxes to hold sweetmeats or writing implements — would be covered with numerous coats of lacquer, each of which had to be left to dry for several months. After a hard crust had formed, the lacquer was carved in diverse designs — not only thematic subjects and ornamental patterns were used, but also many symbols, such as peonies denoting nobility and wealth, rocks and storks denoting longevity, or bats, as bearers of good luck.

Notable among the black, carved Coromandel lacquers to be seen in Room 357 is a large screen of the first half of the eighteenth century. Made of wooden panels, its black-lacquered gesso surface is decorated on one side with brightly coloured scenes of court life and on the other with diverse designs including the traditional bird-and-flower motif.

Enamels

Produced during the Ming (fourteenth — seventeenth centuries) and Ch'ing (eighteenth — early twentieth centuries) dynasties were mag-nificent *cloisonné* enamels.

Current in the eighteenth century were the pieces known in Europe as Canton enamels — as they were made and exported from Canton — though the Chinese themselves called them "European porcelain": apparently because the enamel-painted metal dishes, plates and other wares were fired in the same kilns as porcelain.

Gem, Wood and Ivory Carvings

The more than one thousand carved gem stones in the Hermitage col-lection are amazing not only for the diversity of their realistic subject matter, but also for the craftsmen's ability to compel the often stubborn medium to conform to the shape desired and to derive an artistic ef-fect from its grain and natural colouring.

Paintings by Chinese Artists

The exhibition includes Chinese paintings of various artistic trends. There are examples of ceremonial formal paintings of the Ch'in dyn-

183

asty, which depict the highest officials (183, E-356). All these paintings portray the sitters in rigid conventional postures and are designed according to a single scheme.

Of a much greater interest are works which follow the old tradition of national art, in particular the paintings executed in the Kuo-Hua technique of ink on rice paper or silk. Conspicuous among these are the works done by the two outstanding Chinese painters, Chi'i Pai-shih and Hsü Pei-hung.

E

185

Pictures by Chi'i Pai-shih

A fine connoisseur of nature who displayed great virtuosity in his treatment of animal and plant motifs, Chi'i Pai-shih (1860—1957) rejected any naturalistic copying. Thus in his *Shrimps* (184, E-363) he has scorned detail, but we tend to overlook his use of a white background in place of water and the fact that his crustaceans have less legs than they do in reality; for the painter has been able to convey, with a few rapid strokes of the brush, not only the external appearance of the shrimps but also their characteristic movements, with their entwined legs and feelers, creating a vivid decorative pattern on the long scroll. And the appearance of the Chinese characters above them, which the artist, an eminent calligrapher, has written in such a way that they are somewhat reminiscent of shrimps, makes one view both the inscription and the actual picture as one integral design.

Hsü Pei-Hung. *Geese on a Pond* (185, E-363)

Although Hsü Pei-Hung (1895—1958) mastered painting in oils in the European manner, his talent was fully expressed only when he applied himself to drawing in ink on paper and silk. Thus, *Geese on a Pond*, a picture that he produced in 1932, developed the ancient tradition of the bird-and-flower motif.

Folk Prints

Also on display are numerous woodblock-printed folk pictures, the technique of which originated around the twelfth century. They depict deities, mythological, historical and folklore subjects, as well as beautiful women, theatrical characters and symbols wishing prosperity, health and good luck.

CULTURE AND ART OF INDIA

This relatively small display gives some idea of the diverse range of vivid and original work produced in India from the third century B.C. to the present.

One major contribution to the collection was the group of artistic objects, ranging from the third to eighteenth century, that the Government of India donated to the Hermitage in 1966. It includes a third-century mottled sandstone statue of the stern goddess Durga, spouse of Siva; a tenth-century group of the Siva cult tutelary spirits of fertility, Gomukha and Yaksha, and an exquisite tenth — twelfth century Mithuna (Pair of Lovers), in which traditional features of the Tribjanga (an attitude formed by a threefold bend of the body) art, particularly the presentation of movements, reflecting the suppleness of ancient ritual

187

dances, are merged with a profoundly life-like poetic imagery, inspired
and imbued with sensual, earthly beauty.
Also on show are examples of famous, typically Indian arts and handicrafts, such as ivories, textiles, ivory-inlaid woodwork and damascened steel objects. Attention may be directed to a richly ornamented
screen (186, E-357). There is also a collection of arms and armour of
world significance, several fine ritual stone sculptures going back to
early medieval times, and, finally, paintings, noteworthy among which
are miniatures of the Mughal, Rajput and other schools, as well as *At
the Toilet* by Djamili Roy (187, E-371).

188

CULTURE AND ART OF BYZANTIUM

Mounted in Rooms 381, 381a and 382 is a representative collection of the art and culture of Byzantium, a state with a history of more than a thousand years, from the fourth to fifteenth century. The transition from slave-ownership to feudalism, the emergence of Christianity and the interplay of the local cultures and traditions of the people populating the Empire were all reflected in its art. Highlights of the exhibition are the silverware, ivories and icons.

Silver Vessels

Much of the silver displayed in Room 381a, such as the two embossed dishes, one with the figures of Meleager and Atalanta, and the other

178

189

with Silenus and a dancing Maenad, echoes the shapes and ornamental designs of vessels of classical antiquity, and only a few features such as their schematic, conventional and symbolical nature betray the impact of medieval ideas.

The silver ladle with a chased scene of measuring the level of water in the Nile (188, E-381a) dates from the sixth century. There are, however, objects of an entirely different character. Thus the Latin inscription on a silver paten informs us that it had formerly been a secular dish and then was "ex antiquis renovatum" into an ecclesiastical paten (189, E-381a) by Paternus, bishop of Tomi (now the Rumanian seaport of Constanța). Eclectic, in that it combines features of different styles and times, it carries such antique decorative motifs as the vine running along the entire border of the vessel, birds and animals, as well as such barbarian artistic elements as encrusted coloured paste and gems, while the large Chi-Rho monogram incised on the bottom is of the sixth century. The dish itself bears four control stamps from the reign of Emperor Anastasius (491—518).

190

Consular Diptychs (190, E-381 a)

These diptychs, consisting of two small oblong panels of ivory, hinged like a book, had originally served as scratch-pads — the inner sides having a layer of wax on which a message could be scratched with a *stylus*. Later they were adopted by the Roman Consuls (from whom they derive their name) to send messages to noted persons announcing their election to high office. The Consuls would also distribute bounty among the populace and arrange free entertainment, such as combat between gladiators and wild beasts, and it is this sort of scene that is represented in low relief on the panels. The intricate foreshortening employed to depict the figures in movement conveys the dynamic suspense of this duel between man and animal.

191

E

192

Icon of St. Gregory the Thaumaturgus (191, E-382)

This icon is the finest example of Byzantine art at the Hermitage. Its anonymous twelfth-century painter has created an inspired and deeply human portrait, whose precise draughtsmanship and glowing harmony of colour serve to bring out the coherence and clarity of the symbolic representation.

Icon of Christ Pantocrator (192, E-382)

In this icon, representative of the last short-lived upsurge in fourteenth-century Byzantine art, the bold strokes of white impart depth to the face and heighten the overall emotional impact. Also portrayed are the two donors, the Grand Stratopedarch Alexius and the Grand Primicerion John, who founded the Church of Christ Pantocrator on Mt. Athos. The fact that it has been possible to date the icon on the basis of written records as having been painted in 1363 only enhances its value.

CULTURE AND ART OF IRAN

Sassanian Silver

One of the richest collections in the possession of the Hermitage is that of sumptuous silverware, manufactured in the mighty state ruled by the Sassanid dynasty from the third to seventh century. The silversmiths displayed consummate mastery in their application of such diverse techniques as embossing, casting, gilding, punching and incising. Some magnificent examples of Sassanian work reached faraway places either through barter and trade or as the spoils of war.

Dish with King Shapur II Hunting (193, E-383)

The dish bearing the representation of the Shahanshah (King of Kings) Shapur II (309—379) hunting, unearthed in Viatka (Kirov) Region in 1927, is a masterpiece of Sassanian silverwork. The master craftsman has ably enclosed the dynamic episode within the circular form, drawing upon the sheen of the raised portions to convey depth and dimension. The majesty of the king is accentuated by his attire, tall crown and regal posture on horseback. While the king is represented from three different angles, the lion is depicted twice, rearing as the king aims his bow at it, and prostrate, beneath the horse's hooves. Although small, the scene produces an impression of monumentality.

Persian Bronzes

Persian metalwork of the twelfth — fifteenth centuries is eloquently illustrated by the excellent bronzes exhibited in Room 384. One item is a cauldron, made in 1163, which is inlaid with eight horizontal rows of

194

good-luck inscriptions and scenes depicting backgammon players, horsemen and musicians damascened in silver and red copper.

Of a somewhat later date, 1206, is a bronze aquamanile, amazingly cast in one whole piece despite being in the form of three animals — a zebu cow being suckled by a calf (194, E-384), with a leopard on its back. It also has a surface decoration in incised niello work of minute representations of animals and birds.

Lustre-painted Vase

Among the diverse examples of Persian pottery exhibited in Room 387 is the world's biggest vase with lustre-painted decoration, which is dominated by relief figures of mounted polo players. The rest of the surface is taken up by an ornamental pattern of birds, beasts and plants. The iridescence of the painting, to obtain which the vessel was coated with a special mixture and re-fired, imparts a vivid effect to this vase.

Sassanian Gems and Seals

Carved from precious and semi-precious stones with deities, human figures and portraits, flowers, or scenes of animals in combat, and occasionally accompanied by inscriptions, these engraved gems were used by their owners as seals or were worn as good-luck charms.

Miniature Painting

The basic form of Iranian painting was the miniature which, first employed in the thirteenth century to illuminate manuscripts, subse-

195

quently became an independent field. The chief centres were Tabriz, Shiraz, the Timurid capital of Herat, and, from the 1560s on, the city of Kazwin. Thus *Youth with a Lute* was painted by Sharaf el-Huseini el Yazdhi in 1594 or 1595 in the style of the Kazwin school characterized by the elongated proportions of the figure.

The miniatures of Riza-i-Abbasi (died in 1653), an outstanding exponent of the school of Isfahan, are well illustrative of decorative trends which prevailed in Iranian art at this period. His doublet *Feast* (195, E-392), which is dated 5 January 1612, demonstrates a superb draughtsmanship combined with a vivid colourfulness and extremely expressive composition.

Persian Rugs and Carpets

Exhibited in Rooms 391—393 are several magnificent rugs and carpets woven of the best-quality wools at Kerman, Isfahan and Shiraz. Of extreme sturdiness and with a very close pile, they are richly decorated in bright, festive colours with ornamental and flower motifs sometimes incorporating figures of animals or vases all framed by an arabesque.

CULTURE AND ART OF THE PEOPLES
OF CENTRAL ASIA

The Airtam Frieze (196, E-34)

The bulk of the artefacts shown were unearthed in the process of archaeological excavations in Central Asia. However, the first fragment of the frieze — displayed in Room 34 — depicting a trio of musicians, was found in the Amu-Darya River in 1932. More fragments were discovered when a team of archaeologists went out to investigate the river banks in the vicinity of the first find and dug up the walls of a Buddhist shrine some 1,700 or 1,800 years old. These carvings in high relief on marl limestone reveal a remarkable fusion of local motifs, as expressed in the hair-styles and types of costume jewellery, of Buddhist features, seen in the representation of the musicians and garlands of flowers, and even of antique elements, such as the acanthus leaves — over a long period the art of the peoples populating Central Asia was subject to the powerful influences of the Hellenistic world.

Sogdian Relics

Archaeological excavations have been going on since 1946 on the site of Pyanjikent, which, founded in the fifth century, was devasted by invading Arab forces in the eighth century. The aristocratic quarters unearthed have revealed many exciting artefacts that are to be seen in Room 35, as well as the remains of two pagan temples. Found in one, that had been razed by fire, were charred wooden architectural details and sculptures; in the other wall paintings were discovered. The paintings in Pyanjikent display two distinctive styles, one in monochrome with neat and precise draughtsmanship, the other predominantly polychromatic.

Hall of Elephants (197, E-36)

Although most of the wall paintings that archaeologists have discovered in the seventh- to eighth-century palace of the Bukhara emirs in Varakhsh are of a narrative order, the emphasis in the design of the Hall

of Elephants is on the decorative effect produced by a rhythmical repe-
tition of the single motif of a king enthroned on an elephant that is
being attacked by savage beasts, contrasted with large patches of local
colour — white, yellow and red. Imitating a presumed "Indian" style
of decoration, the local painters drew the elephants, which they had
evidently only heard about, with tusks springing from their lower jaws,
and harnessed them as one would harness a horse.

Blue Room

Displayed in Room 37 are fragments of the décor of what has come to
be termed the Blue Room — namely, the type of wall paintings that
apparently adorned the interior of every rich house in Pyanjikent. The
name derives from the predominantly blue tones used to depict scenes
relating the exploits of the epic hero Rustam — subsequently eulogized
by Firdawsi in his poem *Shah-Nama* (*Book of Kings*). The groups are
composed freely and, despite the diverse foreshortening, the integrity
of the decorative concept has been fully preserved; everything is well
spaced and balanced.

The invading hordes of Genghis Khan, that overran Central Asia in the
1220s, greatly retarded its further economic and cultural advancement.
Only after the victory of united Russian forces on the Field of Kulikovo
in 1380 and the crushing defeats inflicted by Tamerlane was the Golden
Horde toppled.

The Cauldron of Tamerlane (198, E-48)

In Room 48 is a unique two-ton bronze cauldron cast in 1399 by master-
smith Abd-al-Aziz on Tamerlane's express command for the mosque

E

containing the tomb of Khwaja Ahmad Yasevi that was in Yasi, today the city of Turkestan in the Soviet republic of Kazakhstan. The body of this huge vessel, 245 centimetres in diameter, was cast from one intricate, eight-piece mould and embellished on the outside with a fine design in relief. Cast separately were the base and the lotus-shaped handle holds. The Arabic inscriptions which, along with an ornamental design, cover the entire body, state that the cauldron was donated to the mosque by Tamerlane.

Exhibited next to the cauldron are two of the four bronze candle-sticks made on the order of Tamerlane for the same mosque in 1392 and 1397 by the master-smith Izz el-Din.

Mounted in the same room is a highly representative display of mosaic and painted tilework, used in architectural decoration in the times of Tamerlane.

Rooms 50—54 allot considerable space to ethnographical exhibits illustrating Central Asian culture in the sixteenth to nineteenth century.

199

CULTURE AND ART OF URARTU

Karmir-Blur Artefacts

The systematic excavations begun in 1938 under the direction of Boris Piotrovsky on the site of Karmir-Blur (Red Hill), outside the Armenian capital of Yerevan, have yielded priceless material relating to the culture of Urartu, one of the oldest Eastern states, dating back to the ninth — sixth centuries B.C. Unearthed were the ruins of the fort of Teishebaini, built in the seventh century B.C., which was the residence of the viceroys of King Rusa of Urartu, and also remains of the houses that stood at the foot of the hill. Though the citadel was ransacked and burnt by the Scythians early in the sixth century B.C., its lower levels, where provisions had been stored and where artisans had had their workshops, are in a good state of preservation. The artefacts discovered give some idea of the development of the arts and crafts, farming, the art of warfare and writing in ancient Urartu. The bronze figure of a deity (199, E-56) was made in the eighth or seventh century B.C.

 History
of Primitive
Culture

This Hermitage department contains 450,000 items that eloquently describe the development of primitive culture in the territory of what is today the USSR and which span some 400,000 years, from the start of the Paleolithic or Old Stone Age to the rise of the first states.

The origin of the Hermitage's archaeological fund dates back to the early nineteenth century. In the middle of the nineteenth century the Museum acquired the famous Tmutarakan Stone bearing the oldest known Russian inscription, dated 1068 A.D. About the same time the Hermitage received, by transfer from the *Kunstkammer*, the country's oldest archaeological collection, known as the Siberian Collection of Peter the Great, which consisted of numerous gold articles excavated by barrow-diggers in Western Siberia and Kazakhstan in the late seventeenth and early eighteenth centuries.

The collection of Scythian and Sarmatian artefacts as well as those of the Altai nomads constitutes today the main part of the Department's holdings. The bulk of this collection, which in its wealth and variety is unrivalled in the world, is exhibited on the ground floor in Rooms 11—33; all artefacts of gold and other precious materials may be seen in the Special Treasury or Gold Room.

Ground floor

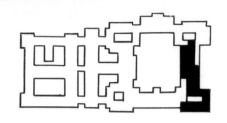

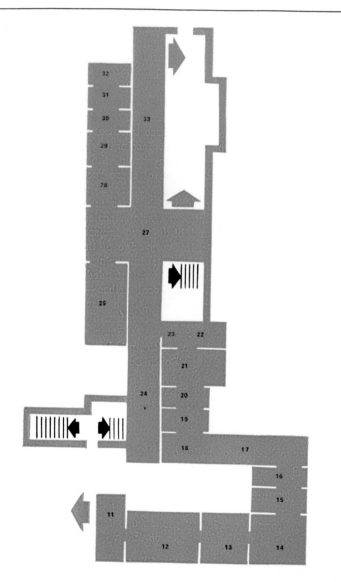

RELICS OF PRIMITIVE CULTURE FOUND
ON THE SOVIET TERRITORY

Satani-dar Hill Celts

P The oldest artefacts ever discovered on the Soviet territory are the celts (chisel-like stone implements) unearthed in 1946—48 on a Lower Paleolithic site at the Satani-dar (Devil's Hill) in Armenia. They comprise two groups which form the largest and finest collection of this kind in the Soviet Union. The first consists of big, crude obsidian implements made 300,000 to 500,000 years ago, when primitive man engaged in early forms of hunting and in the gathering of berries and wild fruit for food. The second group consists of celts of more regular shape and diverse purpose, made of solid basalt, 100,000 to 300,000 years ago, and designed not only to cut and chop but also to pierce, drill and dig.

Lake Onega Petroglyphs

The visitor to Lake Onega will see scattered for some ten kilometres along its Eastern shore a varied assortment of petroglyphs or rock drawings comprising one of the most fascinating displays of Neolithic art in the forest belt of the northern part of the European USSR. In 1935 part of a granite crag with some of these rock drawings was removed and transported to the Hermitage, where it may now be viewed in Room 12. These petroglyphs, which are some 3,000 to 4,000 years old, are schematic line drawings on various scales. The representations of human beings, animals and birds were incised with a stone chisel on rocks that sloped down to the very edge of the water — thus at sunset they seem to spring to life in the shimmering glow reflected on the rippling waves. No doubt, this effect was intended, since the Sun cult dominated the pagan beliefs of the local tribes — as is demonstrated by the solar and lunar signs that have been discovered. It is quite likely that the drawings of boats with oarsmen illustrated the practice of ferrying the dead to the place where "the sun sets" — as, some fifty kilometres away from the shore, in the middle of the lake, archaeologists discovered on Yuzhny Oleny (South Deer) Island a Neolithic burial. Displayed in Room 13 are relics of the Tripolye culture, which, dating back to the late 4,000 — early 2,000 B.C., is the oldest of agrarian cultures in the south-western part of the USSR.

Koban Bronzes

The large collection of relics of what is termed the Koban-Colchis culture consists of finds made in the Northern Caucasus and along the eastern shore of the Black Sea, and particularly from a burial excavated in 1869 near the Ossetian village of Koban — hence the name. The Koban bronzes, which date back to the beginning of the first millennium B.C., consist of elegantly shaped hatchets with geometric designs and representations of deer, snakes and wild beasts (200, P-14).

200

CULTURE AND ART OF THE SCYTHIANS

The Hermitage has the world's largest and richest collection of Scythian antiquities, found in the Southern part of the European USSR. Many of the objects are truly magnificent and without parallel in any other museum. The term "Scythian" is actually an all-embracing definition for the many different tribes that roamed the vast expanses of the region mentioned between the seventh and third centuries B.C., and the representative collection of archaeological and chance finds on display provides an excellent notion of the underivative culture of these ancient tribes.

Stag and *Panther* (201, 202, P-15, 21)

One of the finds made in 1903—4 during the excavation of a barrow near the Kuban Cossack hamlet of Kelermes, where a Scythian chieftain

and his wife had been interred, was a massive gold plaque in the form of a panther. This, and another similar gold plaque, this time in the form of a stag, unearthed in 1897 near the Cossack hamlet of Kostromskaya, are perhaps the most characteristic examples of the Animal Style in Scythian art that have come down to us. Made to adorn the shields of Scythian chieftains, they possess a shamanistic significance; thus the panther's paws are themselves miniature coiled panthers, evidently emphasizing that each paw possesses, as it were, the strength of the animal as a whole, while the tail consists of a string of six panthers. These stylized representations have aptly caught the respective animal's characteristic traits, such as the smooth, cat-like movement of the panther, and the taut, supple body of the bounding stag. Though preferring to exploit the expressive potential of the smooth surfaces and sharp edges, Scythian craftsmen occasionally turned to inlay techniques, using semi-precious stones and coloured paste.

203

Finds from the Scythian Barrows

The numerous Greek-made objects, which the townsfolk of the ancient Pontic colonies gave the Scythians in payment for grain and slaves, illustrate Scythian customs, garments, arms and armour, and ornaments. Discovered during excavations in 1912—13 south of Nikopol beneath the eighteen-metre-high Solokha burial mound of a Scythian chieftain was a unique gold comb (203, P-15), whose handle depicts Scythians in combat, the entire group slightly tapering towards the end. The compact, well-balanced composition, the gradual transition to the teeth of the comb through the two dividing fillets compressing a group of crouching lions between them, all the elements serve to stress the expressive integrity of this remarkable piece of Greek workmanship.

Catering for the tastes of their Scythian clients, Greek craftsmen frequently introduced Scythian motifs into the decoration and design of

the articles made for the steppe nomads. One such item is a fourth-century B.C. goblet of electrum (a gold-and-silver alloy) discovered in the burial of a Scythian chieftain's wife in the Kul-Oba barrow near Kerch. Of a typical antique shape, it has a rosette on its base, alternating bands of strapwork and a raised gadroon design on the lower part of its body and, higher up, scenes in relief of Scythian life, faithfully reproducing their ethnic features, clothing and weapons. Worthy of note is also a magnificent bowl for wine (204, P-15) from the same barrow. The bulk of finds are, however, not of gold, but of bronze, iron and other materials, and perhaps provide a still better idea of Scythian daily life, customs and beliefs. Thus, the artefacts unearthed in the Ulskaya barrow in the Kuban area enable us to imagine the burial rites that the Scythians practised. The apparently rich nobleman interred here, beneath a mound fifteen metres high, was accompanied into the afterworld by four bulls and some four hundred horses — whose bridle bits, frontlets and other harness gear may be seen in Room 15 — all slaughtered and buried with him. Also of interest is the display (mounted in Rooms 18—21) of artefacts illustrating the life and art of the no longer nomadic Scythian farmer.

205

CULTURE AND ART OF THE SARMATIANS

The Sarmatian collection in the possession of the Hermitage is second to none in size and importance.

In the second century B.C. the Sarmatians swooped down from the northern shores of the Caspian Sea upon territories populated by the Scythians and drove them out. Conspicuous among their cultural relics are the finds made in 1864 during excavations of the burial mound of a priestess of the Goddess of Fertility in Novocherkassk on the Lower Don. The gold diadem (205, P-33) is a magnificent example of first-century Sarmatian art. Unlike the Scythians, the Sarmatians did not strive for compact, laconic form, and at times combined various materials to secure a polychromatic effect. Thus, the diadem, topped by an intricately shaped crest with the sacred Tree of Life surrounded by antlered stags and ibexes, is of solid gold inset with garnets, turquoises, corals, pearls and coloured glass, while the small head of an antique Greek goddess, which the Sarmatian craftsman inserted as the diadem's centre-piece, is of amethyst.

The viewer will no doubt be fascinated by the other exhibits, such as a small gold cup with a handle in the form of a she-elk (inset with turquoises, and with its head turned towards the lip of the cup to guard against the intrusion of evil spirits), four scent-bottles and a collar.

CULTURAL RELICS OF THE PEOPLES
OF SOUTHERN SIBERIA:
7th CENTURY — EARLY MIDDLE AGES

The unique display (in Rooms 22—32) of cultural relics of the nomad tribes who roamed the steppes of Southern Siberia in the sixth to fourth centuries B.C., consists of finds made between 1927 and 1954 during excavations of several tombs of tribal chiefs near the village of Tuekta and the Bashadar and Pazyryk gullies in the Altai highlands. As the permafrost has preserved in excellent condition artefacts of stone and metal and has even kept more or less intact items of an organic nature, we are in a position to obtain a well-rounded picture of the nomads way of life and of their culture and art.

Exhibited in Room 26, among the finds made during excavations of the Fifth Pazyryk Tomb, dating from the fifth or fourth century B.C., is a timbered chamber of larch containing a six-metre-long, trough-like cof-

fin in which lie the mummified remains of a tribal chief and his spouse. Many of the discovered artefacts, which were designed to accompany the chief into the underworld are unique, such as the three-metre-high waggon, or chariot, with a rigid front axle, comprised exclusively of wooden elements that could be dismantled and reassembled (206, P-26). Similarly rare is the huge thirty-square-metre *appliqué* felt hanging, which, with another three similar hangings, served to curtain the bier-tent. Of exceptional value is apparently the world's oldest woolen pile carpet decorated with horsemen, animals and ornamental design, which is some 1,700 years older than similar extant carpets, also of Persian workmanship. The finds displayed include musical instruments, horse trappings, masks, pole-tops (207, P-26) and other objects.

The Pazyryk finds, unique both as regards their fine state of preservation and richness, are of world significance, in that, along with the Ba-shadar and Tuekta discoveries, they provide a vast quantity of material for the study of the distant past of the Altai and its peoples.

History of Russian Culture

The Department of the History of Russian Culture is the youngest of the Hermitage's departments. Its formation was directly connected with the important changes in the Museum's policy effected after the October Revolution of 1917, when materials began to be assembled so as to illustrate not only the history of art, as before, but other essential aspects of man's cultural heritage as well. Once the Oriental Department of the History of Primitive Culture had been opened, the need for an exhibition reflecting the historical advance of the Russian people became increasingly evident, all the more so since the Hermitage would be able to present the history of Russian culture in the light of its interrelations with the cultural history of other peoples inhabiting the Soviet Union and many countries outside its borders.

The Department was established in April 1941 and possesses today over 280,000 exhibits, displayed in first-floor Rooms 143—153, 155—190 and 197—198, that trace the history, way of life, and cultural and artistic development of Russia from the sixth to twentieth century.

First
floor

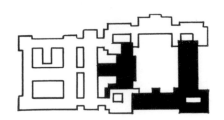

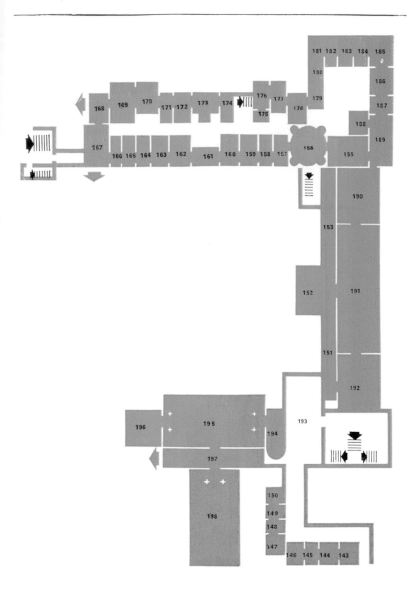

208

RUSSIAN CULTURE: LATE 17th
AND EARLY 18th CENTURIES

The bulk of the exhibition of Russian culture in the Petrine epoch derives from what is known as the Cabinet of Peter the Great which was arranged at the so-called *Kunstkammer* (cabinet of curios) shortly after the Emperor's death and where items associated with him and his age were collected and preserved.

The portrait busts of Peter the Great and his favourite Prince Menshikov, which were modelled by the famous sculptor Carlo Bartolommeo Rastrelli, are of great interest and artistic value. Indeed, the sculptor,

202

who came to Russia at the invitation of the Russian Emperor, and his son Bartolommeo Francesco Rastrelli, designer of the Winter Palace and other superb buildings, largely contributed towards the advancement of Russian culture.

The Bust of Peter the Great by Carlo Bartolommeo Rastrelli (208, R-155)

The best of the sculptured portraits of Peter the Great is the bronze bust that Rastrelli modelled in 1723. The determined turn of the head, the strong, resolute face, the lock of hair that seems disturbed by a breeze, and the asymmetrical, dynamic silhouette with the sharply etched, upturned folds of the ermine-trimmed cloak, angular breastplate and broken diagonal sash of the Order of St. Andrew, all serve to build up a highly romantic image breathing inner power and vigour. The typically Baroque features of Rastrelli's style, such as his monumental and dynamic qualities, emphasized contrasts, elevated pathos and energy, are all brought into play, not only to reveal the sitter's temperament, but also to convey the broader and more general concept of the entire Petrine era with its reforms, hard-fought victories, release from stagnant conservatism, and, nonetheless, its total subordination to the will of Russia's autocratic ruler. The sculptor's model was also used for the iron bust that is currently on view at the Russian Museum in Leningrad. The smaller details of the armour and attire were embossed by the master-engraver Semange under the sculptor's personal supervision and were finished only towards 1729.

R

Rastrelli's earlier bust of Prince Alexander Menshikov, which was done in 1716—17, is also a fine piece of work. It was the first sculpture in Russia to be cast in bronze.

Rotunda and Triumphal Column

The Rotunda (Room 156), which was designed in 1830 by Auguste Montferrand and built after the 1837 fire by Alexander Briullov, has in the centre a reconstruction of the model, designed by Carlo Rastrelli, Nicolas Pineau (1684—1754) and Andrei Nartov, of the Triumphal Column that was to commemorate the victory of Russian arms in the Northern War.

Petrine Prints

The exhibition of Russian engravings in Room 157 demonstrates the great significance that the print assumed in the reign of Peter the Great as a means of popularizing the Emperor's reforms and innovations, disseminating knowledge, and extolling Russia's victories. A typical example is *A View of the Nevsky Prospekt from the Anichkov Palace* by Andrei Martynov (209, R-157).

R

209

Enamelled Miniatures

The art of the portrait miniature, executed in coloured enamel on plaques of gold or a silver-copper alloy, emerged and achieved popularity in the times of Peter the Great. The Emperor would present such miniatures with his portrait as a special mark of distinction, and they were more prized by the recepient than the award of any order. Subsequently in Russia this art developed an independent significance.

Exhibited in Room 158, among the works of the celebrated enameller Grigory Musikiysky (1670 — after 1739), are portraits of Peter the Great shown against the background of the Peter and Paul Fortress and the Holy Trinity Square in St. Petersburg, of Catherine I against the background of the Yekateringof Palace and Park, and of other members of the Emperor's family. Though the portrait as such dominates, the background, besides fulfilling a decorative purpose, also adds to the character study. These enamelled portrait miniatures, painted in bright colours on a white background, are extremely elegant and attractive.

Imperial Turnery

Best known of the eleven lathes from the Imperial Turnery of Peter the Great that the Hermitage has in its possession is the duplicating machine with the first ever mechanically operated carriage or tool clamp to be produced in Russia. It was designed and made in 1718—29 by Andrei Nartov (1690/94—1756), the well-known inventor who headed the Imperial Turnery. To be seen in the next room is a large chandelier of walrus ivory, which was made at the Turnery with the assistance of the Emperor himself, who delighted in taking part in such work.

R

RUSSIAN CULTURE:
MIDDLE AND SECOND HALF OF THE 18th CENTURY

Dominating the exhibition are objects illustrating the advances made over this period in Russian art, and more particularly the applied arts, and also the achievements in science, technology and education.

Early Russian Porcelain. Dmitry Vinogradov

Of special interest and value among the items shown in Room 166 are two small porcelain pieces, a cup with a vine decoration that was slightly deformed during firing, and a snuff-box decorated with two pug dogs admiring their reflection in a mirror. These are the first pieces ever made by the Russian chemist Dmitry Vinogradov (1720—1758) who discovered the secrets of hard-paste porcelain independently of European experts. In 1747 he initiated its manufacture at the St. Petersburg Imperial Porcelain Factory (now the Lomonosov Porcelain Factory in Leningrad). In the possession of the Hermitage are eighty pieces of porcelain that were produced at this factory in Vinogradov's lifetime, among them a service commissioned for the Empress Elizabeth Petrovna in 1756. In Room 169 there is a fascinating exhibition of work produced by Russian inventors and gifted folk craftsmen.

Egg-shaped Clock by Kulibin (210, R-169)

In 1764—67 the self-taught mechanic Ivan Kulibin (1735—1818) completed a complex clock mechanism consisting of 427 parts, which he enclosed within a silver-gilt case the size of a goose egg. The dial and hands

205

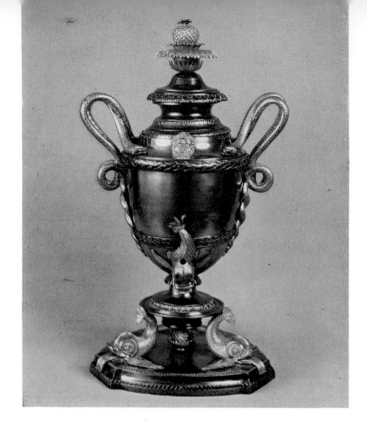

211

are on the underside and there is a small aperture on one side, within which tiny figures act out the scene of the Resurrection of Christ every hour on the hour to the accompaniment of an appropriate thrice-repeated tune. The music box inside not only chimes the quarter-hours and half-hours but also plays at noon a cantata which the maker himself composed in honour of Catherine the Great. For some thirty years Kulibin was supervisor of the mechanical workshops of the St. Petersburg Academy of Sciences.

Tula Steelwork

Remarkable among the numerous exhibits made of steel, such as arms, furniture, chandeliers, caskets, goblets and ink-stands, is the beautiful box made in the eighteenth century of steel and bronze and upholstered with velvet (212, R-174).

By this time the Tula craftsmen had not only mastered various methods of treating metals, such as forging, engraving, etching, chasing and damascening, but also learned to make in steel imitations of diamonds

212

with a large number of facets (up to sixteen). An example of this unusual craft is the casket made by P. Leontyev.

The Hermitage has also a fine collection of famous Tula samovars. One of them, made of steel, with bronze feet in the shape of dolphins, is marked by its original shape and excellence of décor (211, R-174).

The Tomb of Alexander Nevsky (213, R-190)

Taking pride of place in the exhibition of eighteenth- to twentieth-century silverware that is mounted in Room 190 — the former Concert Hall, designed by Vasily Stasov — is the silver sarcophagus of Alexander Nevsky, the great thirteenth-century Russian warrior and statesman. Made at the St. Petersburg Mint in 1747—53, the side reliefs commemorate the victories that Alexander Nevsky won at the Battle of the Neva in 1240, when freeing Pskov in 1242, and when putting the Teutonic Knights to rout on the ice of Lake Chud (Peipus) later in the same year. The ornamental pyramid behind the sarcophagus carries on its apex the sun-burst monogram and conventional representation — there are no authentic portraits in existence — of the prince. Lower down, two effigies of angels, one on each side, hold cartouches inscribed with lines by Mikhail Lomonosov, extolling the distinguished services rendered by Alexander Nevsky, and with the text of the edict that Empress Elizabeth Petrovna promulgated regarding the erection of the

243   memorial. A censer on either side and two decorative supports bearing armour complete this majestic composition which took more than 1,400 kilogrammes of silver to make, and which displays the use of such diverse techniques as casting, embossing and engraving.

Russian Ivories

The traditional Russian handicraft of ivory carving reached its peak in the eighteenth century. Outstanding among the caskets, vases, sculptural groups and portraits carved in low relief on thin sheets of ivory, is the work of two eminent master carvers, Osip Dudin (1714—1785), who was active mainly in St. Petersburg, and Nikolai Vereshchagin (1770 — *ca.* 1814), who lived in Arkhangelsk.

The Dudin Tankard

This handsome object, with its elegant handle, is adorned with medallion portraits, framed by intricately carved openwork, of Russia's rul-

214

ers from Rurik to Catherine the Great. The dark horn setting serves as an excellent background for these cream-tinted silhouettes. As highly decorative are the raised portrait medallions decorating the domed lid, which is topped by minute representations in the round of a crown and orb (Room 214).

The Vereshchagin Vase (214, R-173)

This superb specimen, the biggest of all known objects carved in ivory, is 85 centimetres tall. The craftsman has skilfully blended subtly executed openwork with vertical strips composed of miniscule beads, thereby bringing out handsome proportions of the vase, and has made its focal point a massive garlanded medallion surmounted by the figure of an eagle. In his combined use of the most complex techniques, incorporating sculpture in the round, relief carving, openwork and engraving, Vereshchagin has demonstrated truly consummate mastery and artistic taste.

R

215

Russian Porcelain:
18th and 19th Centuries

The Hermitage possesses as many as 10,000 pieces of Russian-made porcelain. Displayed in Room 173 are items from five large palace services that were produced in the 1780s and 1790s. The sixty-person Arabesque Service, which consists of 973 pieces, had a decoration suggested by the Ancient Roman grotesques that were unearthed in the ruins of Pompeii and Herculaneum. It also included elaborate centre-pieces.

The Yacht Service, whose decoration was intended to extol Russia as a great sea-power, and the Cabinet Service, commissioned for Empress Catherine the Great, each consisted of 800 pieces. The Cabinet Service was adorned with medallions bearing architectural views of Italy — these views, being identified on the reverse of the plates, enabled knowledge of architectural monuments to be put to the test during a banquet.

The porcelain factory that an Englishman, Francis Gardner, set up in the vicinity of Moscow in 1766 — now known as the Dmitrov Porcelain Factory — manufactured not only wares for the general public but also fine porcelain for the Imperial Court, including the celebrated Order services (215, R-172), produced in the 1770s and 1780s and richly decorated with representations of the insignia and sashes of the Orders of St. Andrew the First-called, St. Alexander Nevsky, St. George, and St. Vladimir.

Many porcelain factories produced, in addition to table ware, a large number of small-scale sculptures. The figurine *Woman Carrying Water* (Room 185) was made from a model by the sculptor Stepan Pimenov at the Imperial Porcelain Factory at the beginning of the nineteenth century.

Besides the above-mentioned exhibitions, the Hermitage has the special Gold Room, where valuable objects of Scythian art and culture (7th — 2nd centuries B.C.), ancient Greek articles (5th century B.C.), the jewellery of Western Europe (14th — 19th centuries) and some other precious items are displayed. The Special Treasury of the Department of the East preserves the most valuable objects illustrating the culture and art of the peoples of the region. The Hermitage Department of Numismatics possesses one of the world's largest collections of coins, medals and insignia. Its items are shown in various exhibitions of the Museum.

As the Hermitage cannot exhibit all at once the vast wealth of diverse objects in its possession, temporary displays are systematically arranged of the more valuable and noteworthy items from its vaults. Numerous venues are used, but above all Room 191, which, with a floorspace of 1,150 square metres is the largest of all — also known as the St. Nicholas Hall, it was designed by the architect Vasily Stasov. It is here, and in the Antechamber next door, that collections on loan from other countries are also displayed.

List of the Hermitage Departments

Department of Classical Antiquities

Ground Floor

Ancient Greece: 8th—2nd centuries B.C. *Rooms 100, 111—114, 118, 121*

Ancient cities of the northern Black Sea coast: 7th century B.C.—3rd century A.D. *Rooms 100, 115—117*

Ancient Italy: 7th—2nd centuries B.C. *Room 130*

Ancient Rome: 1st century B.C.—4th century A.D. *Rooms 106—109, 127—129, 131*

Attic vases: 6th—4th centuries B.C. *Room 118*

Carved and engraved gems: 2nd millennium B.C.—4th century A.D. *Room 120*

Department of Western European Art

First Floor

Medieval European applied art: 11th—15th centuries *Room 259*

Italian art: 13th—18th centuries *Rooms 207—238, 241*

Spanish art: 16th—early 19th centuries *Rooms 239—240*

Netherlandish art: 15th—early 17th centuries *Rooms 248, 258, 260—262*

Dutch art: 17th—18th centuries *Rooms 249—257*

Flemish art: 17th century *Rooms 244—247*

German art: 15th—19th centuries *Rooms 263—268*

French art: 15th—19th centuries *Rooms 272—297*

English art: 17th—19th centuries *Rooms 298—302*

Western European arms and armour: 15th—17th centuries *Room 243*

Western European silverware: 17th—18th centuries *Room 282*

Western European porcelain: 18th century *Rooms 269—271*

Western European tapestry *Rooms 200—203*

Western European carved and engraved gems *Room 304*

Second floor

Italian art: 20th century *Room 336*

Belgian art: 19th—20th centuries *Room 335*

Dutch art: 19th—20th centuries *Room 335*

French art: late 19th—20th centuries *Rooms 314—332, 343—350*

Art of Finland, Sweden and Norway: 19th—20th centuries *Room 337*

Art of Hungary, Poland, Rumania and Czechoslovakia: 19th—20th centuries *Room 341*

US art: 20th century *Room 342*

Department of the Culture and Art of the Peoples of the East

Ground floor

Central Asian peoples: 4th millennium B.C.—early 20th century A.D. *Rooms 34—40, 46—54*

Golden Horde: 13th—14th centuries *Rooms 68—69*

Caucasian peoples: 11th century B.C.—19th century A.D. *Rooms 55—66*

Special Oriental Treasury *Rooms 41—45*

Ancient Egypt: 4th millennium B.C.—6th century A.D. *Rooms 80—91*

Ancient Asia Minor (Babylon, Assyria and adjacent states): 4th—1st millennia B.C., Palmyra: 2nd—3rd centuries A.D. *Rooms 92—96*

Second floor

Byzantium: 4th—15th centuries *Rooms 381, 381a, 382*

Near and Middle East (Iran: 3rd—18th centuries, Iraq: 13th—14th centuries, Syria: 13th—14th centuries, Egypt: 7th—15th centuries, and Turkey: 14th—early 19th centuries) *Rooms 383—397*

China: 2nd millennium B.C.—mid-20th century A.D. *Rooms 351—357, 359—364*

Mongolia: 1st century B.C.—19th century A.D. *Rooms 365—367*

India: 3rd century B.C.—20th century A.D. *Rooms 368—371*

Japan: 14th—20th centuries *Rooms 375, 376*

Indonesia: 9th—20th centuries *Room 358*

Department of the History of Russian Culture

First floor

6th—15th century *Rooms 143—150*

15th—17th centuries *Rooms 151—152*

First quarter, 18th century *Rooms 153, 155—161*

Middle and second half, 18th century *Rooms 162—174*

19th century, up to the 1860s *Rooms 175—187*

Russian silverware; 17th—20th centuries *Room 190*

Malachite Room with early 19th-century malachite objects *Room 189*

Memorial Room of Peter the Great *Room 194*

Armorial Hall *Room 195*

War Gallery *Room 197*

St. George Hall *Room 198*

Private Dining Room (room where the bourgeois Provisional Government was arrested in 1917) *Room 188*

Department of the History of Primitive Culture (artefacts found in the territory of the USSR)

Ground floor

Paleolithic and Mesolithic: 500,000—7,000 B.C. *Room 11*

Neolithic, Bronze and Iron Ages: 5,000—500 B.C. *Rooms 12—14, 21*

Scythian culture and art: 7th—3rd centuries B.C. *Rooms 15—21*

Finno-Ugric, Baltic and Slavonic culture and art: 7th century B.C.—12th century A.D. *Room 24*

South Siberian artefacts: 7th century B.C.—early Middle Ages *Rooms 22—23, 26, 28—32*

Culture and art of tribes inhabiting southern steppes: 3rd century B.C.—10th century A.D. *Room 33*

Department of Numismatics

Second floor

Foreign and Russian orders and decorations *Room 399*

Coins *Room 398*

Near Eastern coins: 3rd—20th centuries, and Western European coins: 5th—20th centuries *Room 400*

(Some of the items from the numismatics collection will be found elsewhere in the Museum.)

Index of Artists and Architects

Abd-al-Aziz 187
Amigoni, Jacopo 13
Ast, Balthasar van der
97

Ballin, Claude 114
Bellotto, Bernardo
66, 68
Benois, Leonty 24
Bernini, Lorenzo
63—64
Beyeren, Abraham
van 197
Bloem, Matheus 97
Boucher, François
116, 118—119
Boulle, André-Charles
24, 114—115
Bramante, Donato 24
Briullov, Alexander
19, 203
Brouwer, Adriaen
91, 94
Bruni, Fiodor 24

Campin, Robert
79—80
Canaletto, Antonio
66, 68
Canova, Antonio 64
Caravaggio
(Michelangelo
Merisi) 60, 62, 71
Carracci, Agostino
62
Carracci, Annibale
62, 63
Carracci, Lodovico
62
Cézanne, Paul 138,
139—142
Chardin Jean-
Baptiste-Siméon
121
Chi'i Pai-shih 173,
175
Claesz, Pieter 97
Corot, Jean-Baptiste
Camille 132—133

Correggio, Antonio
100
Cox, James 23
Cranach, Lucas, the
Elder 105, 106—108

Daubigny, Charles
François 128, 129
David, Jacques Louis
123—124
Dawe, George 13
Degas, Edgar 138
Delacroix, Eugène
125—126
Diaz de la Peña,
Narcisse Virgile
128, 129
Dudin, Osip 208—
209
Dupré, Jules 128—
129

El Greco 70
Euphronios 32

Falconet, Étienne-
Maurice 116, 119—
120
Friedrich, Caspar
David 109

Gainsborough,
Thomas 155, 157
Gardner, Francis 211
Gauguin, Paul 138,
143
Giorgione da
Castelfranco 49,
56—57
Golike, Vasily 13
Goya, Francisco de
70, 77
Goyen, Jan van 98
Gros, Antoine Jean
124
Guardi, Francesco
66, 68

Guttuso, Renato 68,
69

Hals, Frans 94
Heda, Willem Claesz
97
Holbein, Ambrosius
105
Holbein, Hans 105
Hooch, Pieter de 94
Houdon, Jean-Antoine
121, 122
Hsü-Pei-hung 173,
175

Ingres, Jean Auguste
Dominique
126—127
Izz el-Din 188

Jacobsz, Dirk 82
Janssens, Pieter 94
Jordaens, Jacob 83,
90

Klausen, Nicholas
13
Klenze, Leo von 27
Krafft, Peter 14
Krüger, Franz 14
Kulibin, Ivan 205—
206

Lebrun, Charles 114
Léger, Fernand
153—154
Le Nain, Matthieu
111, 131
Le Nain, Louis
111—112, 131
Le Nain, Antoine
111, 131
Leontyev, P. 207
Leyden, Lucas van
82
Lippi, Filippino 49

Lorrain, Claude 113
Lysippos 32

Marquet, Albert
152—153
Martini, Simone 48
Matisse, Henri
146—148
Martynov, Andrei
203
Medici, Barnaba 13
Michelangelo
Buonarotti 49, 56
Millet, Jean-François
131
Monet, Claude 133,
139, 140
Montferrand, Auguste
10, 203
Morandi, Giorgio 68
Murillo, Bartolomé
Esteban 70, 75—76
Musikiyisky, Grigory
204

Nartov, Andrei 203,
204
Neer, Aert van der
98

Ostade, Adriaen van
94, 95

Palissy, Bernard
111
Phidias 32, 41
Picasso, Pablo 148—
151
Pimenov, Stepan
211
Pineau, Nicolas 203
Pissarro, Camille
136
Poliakov, Alexander
13
Polykleitos 32
Porcellis, Jan 98

Porcellis, Julius 98
Potter, Paulus 98
Poussin, Nicolas
112—113
Praxiteles 32

Quarenghi, Giacomo
24

Raphael (Raffaello
Sanzio) 26, 49,
52—53, 59, 112
Rastrelli,
Bartolommeo Carlo
202—203
Rastrelli, Francesco
Bartolommeo 9,
203
Rembrandt Harmensz
van Rijn 95, 99—104
Renoir, Auguste 136,
137
Reynolds, Joshua
155—157
Ribera, José de 70,
71
Riza-i-Abbasi 185
Rodin, Auguste 144
Rossi, Carlo 13, 14
Rousseau, Théodore
128
Roy, Djamili 177
Rubens, Peter Paul
83—87, 89
Ruisdael, Jacob van
98
Ruysdael, Salomon
van 98

Scotti, Pietro 13
Semange 203
Sharaf el-Huseini el
Yazdhi 185
Sisley, Alfred 136
Skopas 32
Snyders, Frans 83,
91
Stakenschneider,
Andrei 20, 24

Stasov, Vasily 9, 10,
13, 14, 16, 27, 207,
211
Steen, Jan 94

Teniers, David, the
Younger 92—93
Terborch, Gerard 94
Terebenev, Alexander
27
Tiepolo, Giovanni
Battista 66—67
Tiziani, Gasparo 10
Titian (Tiziano
Vecellio) 49, 58—
60, 100
Troyon, Constant
128, 131

Vallin de la Mothe,
Jean-Baptiste 20
Van Dyck, Anthony
83, 88—90
Van Gogh, Vincent
138, 142—143
Velázquez, Diego de
Silva y 70, 73—74
Velten, Yuri 20, 24
Vereshchagin, Nikolai
208, 209
Vinci, Leonardo da
24, 49, 50—52, 59,
105
Vinogradov, Dmitry
205

Watteau, Antoine
117
Wedgwood, Josiah
158
Weyden, Rogier Van
der 80—81

Yefimov, Nikolai 27

Zurbarán, Francisco
de 70, 72

ЭРМИТАЖ

**Иллюстрированный
путеводитель
(на английском языке)**

Автор-составитель
Юрий Горациевич Шапиро

Фотографы **Л. Б. Богданов,
В. С. Теребенин**

Редакторы **Н. И. Василевская,
Н. Г. Моисеева**

Редактор английского текста
В. А. Фатеев

Художественный редактор
С. М. Малахов

Технические редакторы
Т. В. Езерская, Н. К. Соколова

Корректор **Е. Ю. Харькова**

ИБ № 1282. Сдано в набор 10.11.82.
Подписано в печать 15.06.83. Формат
60×84¹/₁₆. Бумага мелованная. Гарни-
тура обыкновенная. Печать высокая.
Усл. печ. л. 12,56. Уч.-изд. л. 13,13.
Тираж 50 000. Заказ 7436. Изд. № 2610.
Цена 3 р. 30 к.
Издательство ,,Аврора". 191065, Ле-
нинград, Невский пр., 7/9. Ордена
Трудового Красного Знамени ленин-
градская типография № 3 имени
Ивана Федорова Союзполиграфпрома
при Государственном комитете СССР
по делам издательств, полиграфии и
книжной торговли. 191126, Ленин-
град, Звенигородская ул., 11

USSR
Leningrad, 193000
St. Isaac's square, 11
"Intourist" office
English group
SVETLANA BULANOVA